In an era when major change initiatives cost millions of dollars and impact tens of thousands of people, adding professional change management expertise to a project team is a no-brainer investment. By engaging Dr. Killpack and using the same tools and techniques provided in this book, I was better able to leverage and enhance my overall leadership effectiveness and successfully sponsor a large, enterprise-wide change transformation.

Steve Gordon, MD
National Healthcare Principal, Point B

Leading or impacted by change in healthcare? This book is for you! This immensely practical guide is a must-read for leaders, project team members, clinicians, and front line staff alike. Keely delivers useful advice and tools that will improve your change game immediately. Take the mystery out of change and build confidence with Keely as your coach.

Claire McCarthy, MA, FHIMSS, CCMP
2010 HIMSS Book of the Year Co-Author

Keely and her change team were instrumental in the success of the project. They were able to bridge the gap between Implementation (IT) and the operational teams to ensure the necessary change management factors were considered and executed. This allowed transparency with the end user and the leadership base, which was a major contributing factor to the overall success of the project.

Keely was an excellent resource to work with throughout the course of the project. She brought key change management expertise and drove communication, change management, and system adoption experience that was invaluable to the project.

Marc Movrich
Implementation Services Director, Epic Systems

Change Rx for Healthcare
Your Prescription for Leading Change

Change Rx for Healthcare
Your Prescription for Leading Change

Keely Killpack, PhD

CRC Press
Taylor & Francis Group
Boca Raton London New York

CRC Press is an imprint of the
Taylor & Francis Group, an **informa** business
A PRODUCTIVITY PRESS BOOK

CRC Press
Taylor & Francis Group
6000 Broken Sound Parkway NW, Suite 300
Boca Raton, FL 33487-2742

Library of Congress Cataloging-in-Publication Data

Names: Killpack, Keely, author.
Title: Change Rx for Healthcare : Your Prescription for Leading Change /
Keely Killpack.
Description: Boca Raton : Taylor & Francis, 2017.
Identifiers: LCCN 2016047022| ISBN 9781498774468 (paperback : alk. paper) |
ISBN 9781498774475 (eBook)
Subjects: | MESH: Health Services Administration | Organizational Innovation
| Health Personnel--organization & administration | Adaptation,
Psychological | Leadership | United States
Classification: LCC RA971 | NLM W 84 AA1 | DDC 362.11--dc23
LC record available at https://lccn.loc.gov/2016047022

Visit the Taylor & Francis Web site at
http://www.taylorandfrancis.com

and the CRC Press Web site at
http://www.crcpress.com

This book is dedicated to you, reader! If you are changing healthcare, I wrote this book for you. Administrators, clinicians, consultants, doctors, insurance, pharma, technology, and more—thank you for your compassion and dedication to our health! My gift to you in the pages ahead are some thoughts, psychology, and tools to make changes in your slice of this world a little easier, I promise.

Contents

SECTION III EXECUTIVES DRIVING CHANGE

SECTION IV LEADERS AND PEOPLE ON PROJECTS MAKING CHANGE

SECTION V PHYSICIAN SUPPORT THROUGH CHANGE

SECTION VI THE CHANGE ADOPTION PROFESSION

Preface

Are you making big changes in your healthcare organization? This book will help any executive, physician, leader, project member or consultant, or change management professional become more familiar with the science of change and tools that make it faster and easier. *Change Rx for Healthcare: Your Prescription for Leading Change* helps readers get their minds around the big drivers of change in healthcare and why people need support to successfully adopt large-scale changes. Practical insights for executives and physicians are discussed, as well as an incredible success story about a large, transformational change implementing Epic's electronic health record (EHR) platform. Readers will find a collection of best practice tools and innovative change adoption tips showcased, which are also downloadable templates (http://www.ChangeRxBook.com)! Written by a seasoned change management strategist, *Change Rx for Healthcare: Your Prescription for Leading Change* also leverages adult learning theory, so there are plenty of hidden gems and activities included to apply the content immediately to your professional environment.

Acknowledgments

It truly takes a village to create a book and I'd like to thank my people for the countless supportive acts and helpful ways they contributed to this book coming alive. I could not have done this work alone and because of each of you, dreams do come true. Thank you so much for helping me become an author!

- **Change and Adoption Team Members**—Julia Antonich, Sarah Bruce, Mary Anne Hannum, Kate Hartwig, Linda Hornli, Daniel McGinnis, Tracy Oulman, Beth Quartarolo, Sharon Moore, Mary Beth Saddoris, Marie Weissman, Jerry Zygmuntowicz—Thanks for trusting my leadership, doing such incredible work and taking the leap together!
- **Steve Gordon, MD** for hiring me, valuing my expertise, and being such an inspiring executive!
- **Greg and Judith Hathaway** for being the most inspirational and supportive parents on Earth!
- **Joanna Horowitz** for the marketing and branding support!

- **Jason and Liz Killpack** for being the world's best brother and sister-in-law and helping in a myriad of ways I will never reveal!
- **Laurie Lemieux** for hiring me, giving me such sage advice, and for the strategic support!
- **Claire McCarthy** for all the publishing help, friendship, and endless mentorship!
- **Kris Mednansky** for taking on a new author and being so supportive all along the way!
- **Beth Montag-Schmaltz** for giving me courage to take a leap and become an author!
- **Marc Movrich** for being such a fun leader and great collaborative partner!
- **Lisa Rebagliati** for editorial support and subject matter feedback!
- **Kaytlyn Sanders** for the personal support and coaching!
- **Alison Taylor** for all the advice, personal support, and editing genius!
- **Travis Tietsema** for believing in my work from the beginning and for all the happiness you brought to this journey!
- **Michael Uribe** for your friendship and confidence in my abilities!
- **Alex Yiznitsky** for all the marketing and branding support!

About the Author

Keely Killpack, PhD, is a professional change management strategist and change adoption expert with more than a dozen years of experience supporting diverse client organizations through transformational changes. Keely is known for her highly collaborative approach to large-scale change adoption in healthcare, retail, government agencies, energy, and transportation. She has created and successfully implemented three complete change management methodologies and toolkits.

Keely earned a PhD in organizational psychology and is an active leader in the change management industry. She is a founding member of the global Association of Change Management Professionals (ACMP), their Pacific Northwest Chapter, and their Thought Leadership Team. Keely has presented her ideas and inspiring client success stories at numerous international and national conferences throughout the last decade. Keely also served as an adjunct professor at Presidio Graduate School, teaching courses in change, communication, and leadership.

Introduction

Everywhere you look in healthcare, changes are emerging. Lots of them. You know how disruptive change can be and yet the pressure to keep productivity up and staffing lean is ever present. Did you know there are proven methods, activities, and tools to help make change and adoption a little easier? There is an entire industry focused on the work of making the change experience as fast and easy as possible. These skilled practitioners work in most global industries and use their skills in psychology and proven change methodologies to help companies like yours and the people in them adopt changes more efficiently.

If you are part of a large-scale change effort or being asked to help shepherd one at your organization, some expert support in managing change could be invaluable. In this book, you will find several of the essential tools used by change management professionals like me and critical insights to help you support change more effectively. I'm also sharing the story of one of the most successful electronic health record (EHR) implementation and transformational changes in recent history.

Adults learn best by applying what they learn at the time it is relevant. To help you get the most learning out of this book, I have provided opportunities for you to directly apply the concepts in your work or activities that will help advance your thinking about change. These opportunities are provided in **Your Prescription for Leading Change** at the beginning of each section, and in **Call to action!** boxes that appear throughout many of the chapters. **Call to action!** boxes will ask you to reflect, jot notes, circle, score concepts or other engaging activities. Changing behavior takes action and effort, so readers of this book should expect nothing less from a change book.

Lastly, this book is organized in sections so you can customize your reading experience as you wish. The Table of Contents provides all the specifics, but it's worth mentioning here as well that the first two sections are conceptual sections that set the context for the book: change being the only constant in healthcare and the value of investing in change adoption. The next four sections are organized by role: executives driving change, people making change, physician support through change, and change adoption professionals. The last section contains some best practices for successful change adoption for every reader's delight. **Enjoy!**

I

CHANGE, THE
ONLY CONSTANT
IN HEALTHCARE

Overview: This section synthesizes the many drivers of change, why changes in healthcare are more often and more complex, and provides some comparison to other industries that have embarked on similar transformations. Common language and definitions for terms are introduced, and author credibility is also established.

Your Prescription for Leading Change: Here are some immediate steps you can take to adopt the ideas in this section.

■ Identify one to two initiatives your company is working on to adapt to the changes in healthcare or to respond to the market.

- Create a list of all the drivers of change for your job type, specialty/practice, or organization. Reflect on each of them and identify the next step toward making the desired change.
- Share key highlights of this section with your colleagues. Maximize your effort in reading this section so it benefits your unit, department, or clinic colleagues!

Chapter 1

Experience Counts When Adopting Change

Change. It is everywhere and now it is constant. Time and again, we are asked to change the ways we do things in our lives and particularly at work. In spite of changing our behavior repeatedly, it does not seem to make adopting change any easier. With changes coming faster and with more frequency in healthcare, we need to get better at adopting change. This book is about helping people who work in healthcare adopt changes more effectively. If you work in healthcare and are impacted by change in any way, keep reading! This book is written just for you.

Let's start by personalizing this book. I encourage you to take a moment to reflect upon changes you have been a part of and ask yourself the following questions. Feel free to jot your answers down right here in the book; it will help make the concepts stick! Go ahead and consider:

- Did those changes go smoothly?
- Did I embrace or resist those changes? Did our employees embrace or resist them?
- Did we reap all the benefits we targeted in our business case? Do I know what benefits we were seeking?
- If we had to do them over again, would I recommend that we reach out to ask a change management expert to help us make the changes more efficiently?

After more than a dozen years working as a change management consultant and strategist, I can tell you that almost all companies who have experienced big, complex changes answer these questions in similar ways:

- Some changes went fairly smooth; most were bumpier than expected.
- Most employees eventually adopted the changes; some had a harder time than others.
- Some employees liked the idea of the changes right up front; many had to be convinced of the value of the change to varying degrees.
- The benefits had to be clearly and repeatedly discussed for employees to commit to the change.
- For most changes, the business case had clear benefits tied to employee adoption and process efficiencies,

but the measurement and the actual value achieved are not known.

■ There's a general mystery around managing change: what it means, what people in the change management field actually do, how to determine the scope of change support that might be needed, and how to find this type of talent.

Comparing your notes to my experiences above, you can see how common or exceptional your change experiences have been in the past. Thinking along these lines, we can begin to consider ways we can improve our change experiences in the future or current change initiatives that may be happening now.

The truth is that most of the time we make decisions based on our available time and resources. During tax season, we may choose to do our taxes ourselves or to hire an accountant. In spring, we may put all our weekend free time into yardwork, or hire a landscaper to help us get the outdoor space set up for summer. When organizations decide to embark on a large-scale change initiative, they may contract experts in the type of change (technology experts, workflow analysts, etc.) or they may use internal employees—most often a mix of both.

When a change initiative or project is going to significantly change the way we operate, most companies acknowledge this will be a burden to employees and that "the people side of change" is something we need to address. Despite knowing this is a real burden to our employees and our productivity, healthcare companies often choose not to budget change experts who can address change and make it faster and easier. I want you to know that for decades, many other industries have been investing in change experts and recognize the value and benefits of managing the people side of change.

Change management is the process, tools, and techniques used to manage the people side of change and achieve a desired business outcome. Change management incorporates organizational tools that can be utilized to help individuals make successful personal transitions resulting in the adoption and realization of change.[1]

Change management professionals work in many industries all over the world, have standards and certifications for our practice, and have a global professional association. More importantly, we can help scope the magnitude of change, develop strategies, and execute work to best support the people who need to change in appropriate ways for any organization. If you haven't worked with one of us yet, consider reading this book as your gateway into our industry!

I mention change management in the industry and its practitioners because we all know that healthcare is changing rapidly and in really big ways. In most cases, it's worth the time and investment to discuss the change initiatives at your organization with a professional change expert. But not to worry, if you don't have extra budget or are still skeptical, keep reading.

The rest of this book clarifies why changes in healthcare are constant and profound. It will highlight a case study of a very successful, large, transformational change and provides advice, actions, and best practices for any reader to help make adopting changes easier. You will also see many tools throughout this book. These are the actual tools used in the case study of a large-scale transformation, and we have made it easy to leverage these tools to create your own. Full color tool templates, which include the sample, instructions, and template forms, are available for download on the website http://www.ChangeRxBook.com.

Chapter 2

Paradigm Shift: Patient as Consumer

A wise doctor once explained to me that healthcare has long been a blend of change and constancy. He said that critical elements of our work like forms, codes, devices, and drug treatments continuously evolve, while annual checkups and trips to emergency rooms have largely stayed the same.

The longer anything stays the same, the harder it is to change when the time comes. Consider for just a moment how hard it would be to drive on the other side of the road or to eat with your nondominant hand holding your fork or even to sleep in a completely new position from now on.

Healthcare is being pressured to change in a few very important ways and all at once. Why? Largely because we have generally operated in the same ways for a long time while changes in the marketplace have been gaining momentum over the years and are now timely. To be more specific, there are three main drivers of change in healthcare today:

1. **Payment/policy**—examples include Affordable Care Act requirements and revenue shifts with the increase in patients with Medicare/Medicaid coverage and consolidation of markets.
2. **Technology innovations**—examples include electronic health records, genome testing, and advancements in drug therapies.
3. **Care model or delivery**—examples include targeted cancer treatments, opioid dependency, and orthoscopic or transcatheter procedures.

With all of these change drivers influencing our industry's future, organizational leaders are working overtime to strategize how we need to change our operations in order to stay competitive, provide quality service, and remain profitable. The good news is that changes that address any of these drivers have only one customer to consider: the patient.

The patient has always been in the center of our work and continues to be the focus of our industry. But now the patient also drives change. Patients influence change in our organizations in a few ways:

1. More people are insured, so patient demand is high and the supply of providers is low. This drives resourcing/talent searches and competitive hiring practices.
2. More information is available to patients than ever before: drug therapies, alternative therapies, physician ratings, care experience feedback, cost estimates for some

procedures, insurance coverage comparisons, and more. Our patients are more informed, which means we have to be more informed and more open to learning and adapting our business, our prices, our patient care experience, and collaborating with partners like never before.

3. Much of the world's business is becoming virtual, real time, and self-servicing. People expect immediate, current access to all of their data, direct access to companies they employ for any service, and on-demand availability of support they need to solve their challenges. There are not a lot of industries left where you have to wait for 2 weeks or more to talk to someone about something you urgently want to pay them to fix.

If we view the patient as a consumer of our services, we begin to see why we need to change our industry in a myriad of ways and quickly. Our patients' tolerance for waiting is shrinking, because we live in an on-demand world. Our patients' demand for information and treatment options is growing because their health is more complex and there is so much information available. Our patients' ability to make decisions based on cost comparisons or the breadth of our treatment offerings can no longer be stifled by our lack of transparency and data sharing.

Healthcare is not alone. Many other industries have transformed because of these three drivers and consumer demand. Table 2.1 shows just a few examples that illustrate how significant industry change becomes, when they are focused on the status quo for too long.

Table 2.1 Examples of Industry Transformations

Industry	Description	Drivers of Change
Banking	The 2008 recession exposed financial market fraud, upended banking, lending practices, and real estate industries.	**Payment/policy**—new regulations, limits
		Tech innovation—online mortgage applications, regulatory checks in electronic processing steps
		Service delivery—increased transparency, penalties for abuse, fixed price for vendor services
High Tech	Throughout the 2000s, the transition from laptops and PCs with programs to mobile devices with easier to use apps and interfaces to everything.	**Payment/policy**—secure online $$ transactions
		Tech innovation—apps, cloud storage, streaming
		Service delivery—easier for the user, mobile friendly, and increased accessibility
Media	The 2005 uprising of social media transformed the TV, print, and advertising industries. Using celebrity and consumer opinions to sell brands and influence lifestyle.	**Payment/policy**—sponsorship of a product more powerful than the product itself
		Tech innovation—all social media platforms, streaming video/cable TV alternatives
		Service delivery—endless free to the consumer options for digital marketing

(Continued)

Table 2.1 (Continued)   Examples of Industry Transformations

Industry	Description	Drivers of Change
Ride Sharing	Since 2010, the launch of online transportation network companies (like Uber and Lyft) has changed the value of a car and the way people get around. This shift is also pushing change in taxi, limo, and car service companies.	**Payment/policy**—no cash or point of sale transaction
		Tech innovation—smart phone app only
		Service delivery—automated, real-time estimated cost and driver tracking, no time wasted in transacting for service

Do you remember experiencing these transformations as a consumer? For many of us, these changes were bumpy and at times chaotic. Information was coming at us from all directions, in all flavors, and we had skepticism about all of it. Then followed a lack of trust and loss of confidence in leaders and companies we had known and a growing interest in the new and seemingly better. I think many of us realized the power and influence we can have as consumers. Despite these industries having a lot of practice at changing things over time, they were not very swift or efficient at adopting these bigger transformations.

So, with our patients as consumers and other drivers of change influencing our industry, we know that we will have to adapt and that means significant, transformative change. Let's turn our attention to the biggest policy/payment change in American history, the Affordable Care Act (ACA or Obamacare). It deserves a whole chapter of its own based on all the changes it has brought to our industry already.

Call to action!
Breathe. Deep this time, like you mean it. Ah…one more time. Relaxed readers are more focused and more likely to retain what they are reading. One more deep breath. Okay, carry on!

Chapter 3

Drivers of Change: Legislation Basics

Healthcare sometimes feels like a place where change happens all the time. Anyone who has a long tenure in healthcare or knows a veteran in the field will tell you this industry changes all the time, and it looks nothing like it did 30, 20, even 10 years ago. This is because most of our essential healthcare tools have evolved over time: devices, drugs, documents/forms, insurance codes, regulations, software, tests, and workflows. Taken separately, we can easily see changes to each of these essentials and how these changes have evolved healthcare practice. But that's not the same as the whole industry transforming like the banking, high tech, media, and transportation examples in the previous chapter. The buildup of all these incremental changes to our essential tools has been significant, but not transformational. That's important because we have had a lot of practice changing things on a smaller scale, and yet we lack the grace and skill to transform quickly and easily.

Healthcare is transforming now and that is in large part because of the Affordable Care Act (ACA or Obamacare). You don't need to be a legislation expert, but it helps to know in broad terms how Obamacare is pushing healthcare to transform. Beyond these current drivers of change, we also need to consider that our country's leaders are planning even more governmental changes to our industry. Until the next set of changes are realized on Capitol Hill, we should still be working hard to serve our patients and adapt to their expectations and our market landscape.

The following is a brief synopsis of the key areas of change triggered by Obamacare. If these areas are part of your company's strategic priorities, transformative change is headed your way!

■ **Patient accountability**—The right and responsibility for patients to have complete and easy access to their health records and all it contains. As a consumer of healthcare services, this is why patients are asked to validate information in our chart and why we get copies of our treatment plans and visit summaries each time we visit a healthcare facility.

■ **Transparency of health record**—Access and review of data, decisions, notes, opinions, and treatments for diagnosis and illness by all practitioners who treat or care for a patient. This increases the accountability of the caregiving staff and can influence a myriad of treatment decisions when more data are available.

■ **Best practices and reporting**—The requirement to track, analyze, and report data around costs of care, drug regimens, hospital borne illness, insurance coverage/payments, surgery results, treatment outcomes, and more. This is a huge benefit to the healthcare consumer and is bringing monumental changes to all corners of healthcare:

- Standardizing costs of all drugs, procedures, and treatments
- Increasing every patient's chances at a successful recovery for whatever ails them
- Increasing knowledge sharing among physicians regardless of specialty
- Helping policy regulators make more informed decisions around health services
- Helping administrators see their operational strengths and challenges more clearly, so they can keep costs down and focus their resources on the right improvement initiatives

■ **Population health**—The focus on the health of our geographical communities and providing government incentives to help communities get healthier, not just healing them when they are sick. This shift in thinking and financial benefits from sickness to wellness, and from each patient to a whole community of people, are monumental shifts for healthcare. Almost all healthcare companies you can think of are still struggling to adapt or transform in these ways. Measuring health instead of illness recovery, motivating our consumers to want to be healthier, collaborating with competitors, and making new partnerships to increase wellness and access to healthier products and lifestyle choices are indeed a major transformation under construction in many ways.

■ **Revenue**—The revenue model is shifting from acute inpatient care to outpatient services, and the smaller profit margins that accompany outpatient services. Mandatory insurance coverage has meant that millions more people are going to see a doctor before they need an emergency room visit. This has resulted in many more office visits and more people staying healthy. Revenue is also impacted by the large increase in federally funded insurance plans (Medicare, etc.), which pay less for services than any other type of insurance. The more visits from consumers with this type of coverage, the smaller the revenue for each of their encounters.

■ **Service standards**—Whenever you shine a spotlight on something, more people pay attention. This can create service expectations that influence markets and organizational success. In healthcare, we have 20 million more consumers than ever before. Shortages of staff and longer wait times are now the industry standard. We have Obamacare consistently under scrutiny in Congress, which is also bringing the inconsistencies in the cost of care to the surface for drugs, procedures, and insurance coverage. For many consumers, their expectations for service are not being met adequately, and they are shopping around for improved alternatives.

We have many forces pushing healthcare to transform: the three drivers of change, the patient as consumer and their expectations, as well as Obamacare legislation and all it brings to market. Most companies are working on change initiatives in many of these areas, and as a result, we are experiencing the chaos and uncertainty of change. While we focus on transforming our industry, we also continue to make updates to our essential tools: devices, drugs, documents/forms, insurance codes, regulations, software, tests, and workflows.

Is the scale of change in healthcare clearer now? The next section of this book brings solutions to these change concepts. Some basic change concepts are discussed, as well as a very compelling success story of an organization that recently transformed its entire health system by implementing a new electronic health record platform and standardizing its operations.

Inspired by something you read?
Tweet about it **@DrKeelyK** or **#ChangeRxBook**

II

THE VALUE OF INVESTING IN CHANGE ADOPTION

Overview: This section clarifies some basic change terminology and provides a case study of a very successful change transformation. The success story of a medium-sized health system's adoption of an electronic health record (EHR) platform and standardized processes is described. Stories are told about both the experience of the organization and also the successes working with the EHR vendor, Epic.

Your Prescription for Leading Change: Here are some immediate steps you can take to adopt the ideas in this section.

- Familiarize yourself with the change terminology and use it in your discussions about change.
- Compare this case study to your organization's EHR implementation and identify the similarities and differences.
- Use this comparison to determine if opportunities to invest in change adoption support exist in your organization. Clean up your notes and have a conversation about your thoughts and ideas with the appropriate decision maker.

Chapter 4

Managing, Transforming, and Adopting Change

We know that healthcare is a firestorm of change right now and the key drivers for these changes, but what about your organization and whatever changes are happening there? If you are leading or are involved in a change initiative of any kind, it's important to be able to accurately use basic change concepts. There are a few terms you are going to hear and say from now on, so let's clarify a few things before we dive in:

- **Change initiative**—Any project, program, or initiative that requires *people* to do their jobs differently in some way. Examples include a department reorganization, installing new software, or learning a new process for doing something familiar like annual performance evaluations.

- **Standard change or transformational change**— Many standard changes happen in the workplace predictably (examples include new devices, enhanced forms, and updated insurance codes). Other changes are transformational. They are big and complex, and bring change to almost everything at work. Examples are as follows:
  - A new electronic health record system
  - A new surgical robot that replaces the one that all the surgical staff knew how to use
  - A merger with another organization
  - A new quality initiative that standardizes care plans across all departments of a hospital
- **Change involves emotions**—When a change is so disruptive that it causes negative emotional responses from the people impacted, the change initiative could be at risk of failing. Negative emotional responses can cause people to resist the change. If you believe there could be risk because of people's emotional response to the change, consider that a transformational change. A transformational change requires people to think and feel differently.[2] In order to transform and feel differently, skilled change experts are likely needed to help.
- **Change management and change adoption**— Change management is a global industry. Professionals in this field incorporate psychology and organizational tools that help individuals make successful personal transitions resulting in the adoption and realization of

change.[1] Organizations invest in people with these skills for transformational changes, the big changes that require employees to think, feel, and behave significantly differently. People in this profession that have these skills and do this work come by many names—*Change Management Practitioners, Change Management Professionals, Change Consultants, Change Managers*, etc. But skilled Change Management people really are *Change Adoption Professionals*. They help companies, their leaders and employees, navigate the change experience and adopt changes that are being implemented so the intended business value is realized. It's not really about managing the actual change (that's what project managers do); it's about helping people to get ready and adopt the change with minimal disruption and discomfort. **I will continue to use the words change adoption to better clarify this work.** *NOTE: Change management also has a different meaning in technology, which is another reason to refer to the people side of change as change adoption.*

These concepts are used throughout the rest of this book and should be part of any planning discussions about making changes in an organization. Section 6 also reveals much more about the science, methodologies, tools, and measurements that Change Adoption Professionals use. The Appendix at the end of the book includes these and more concepts for quick reference.

Now that we have some common language around change terms, do you want to hear a story? A really good one about a place that invested in a change adoption team and transformed how every single person works and treats one another in times of large-scale change? It's worth the read, I promise.

Chapter 5

Success Story: Transforming Healing Neighbors Healthcare

I'd like to share a recent personal story, the case study of an organization we will call Healing Neighbors Healthcare. Healing Neighbors Healthcare (HNH) is a medium-sized, healthcare system that spent more than 3 years changing from a holding company containing hospitals, clinics, and labs to an integrated healthcare system supporting population health services in three states.

Healing Neighbors Healthcare (HNH) is like many healthcare systems across the country. It's a not-for-profit healthcare system composed of large medical centers, small critical access hospitals, medical clinics of all specialties, and laboratories. They employ more than 15,000 staff and almost 1000 physicians perform care in their facilities. Like many healthcare systems, it evolved from a single entity to a collection of entities over time. Once they amassed 10 hospitals and about 120 clinics spread across three states, the organization began making the transition to become a clinically integrated system, strengthening the relationships between its regions, entities, employees, and physicians. They also began standardizing workflows, order sets, medication formularies, care processes, and policies. Administrative operations were centralized, and a decision was made to transition all outpatient, inpatient, and business office functions to a single electronic health record (EHR) and Epic was the chosen vendor.

The new EHR and standardized work processes were implemented in four phases:

1. **Outpatient clinics:** ~80 medical clinics total, all specialties, in all geographic locations
2. **Network A:** Two regionally located hospitals (1 large, 1 medium), 15 clinics, 2 labs, and all centralized revenue functions
3. **Network B:** Four regionally located hospitals (1 large, 1 medium, 2 critical access), 15 clinics, 4 labs, and additional centralized revenue staff
4. **Network C:** Four regionally located hospitals (1 large, 1 medium, 2 critical access), 10 clinics, 5 labs, and additional centralized revenue staff

Figure 5.1 is the strategic timeline. This at-a-glance graphic was created to communicate the implementation schedule for all four phases.

To effectively navigate this large scale, transformational change, HNH invested in a Change Adoption Team. The

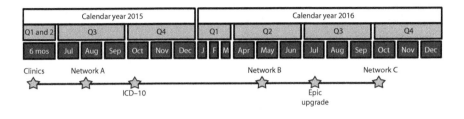

Figure 5.1   At-a-glance timeline.

10-member team was distributed across all locations, and its members were seasoned, experienced change management practitioners. The Change Adoption Team was part of Operational Excellence and reported directly to the Senior Vice President of Operations. It was integral to the team's success to have a direct link to the company's most senior executives and to be involved in strategic decision making and priority setting. I'll cover this in more detail in Section 3—Executives Driving Change.

   The team's focus was to develop the organization's change adoption methodology, change leadership capabilities, and help the organization achieve measurable value from adopting the largest strategic initiative it had undertaken to date. Our work was predominately focused on the implementation of system-wide new electronic health record (EHR), standardized work processes, and computerized physician order entry. Remarkably, the team was able to achieve all of this work in under 3 years and with more success than any other health system to date.

The value of the change adoption effort was clearly realized in a few amazing ways:

- Every executive in each location engaged directly with the Change Adoption Team and learned basic change leadership skills.
- 98% of executives and senior leaders participated in the EHR implementations and demonstrated their newly learned basic change leadership skills.
- Hundreds of thousands in cost savings were realized during implementations due to the collaborative attitudes and increased speed of adoption.
- Standardized workflows were adopted immediately and were successfully executed in almost all departments and locations.
- Adoption of physician order entry was immediate and maintained above 95% in all implementation locations.
- Physicians and leaders in all locations reported feeling more supported and connected to the rest of the organization through this experience compared to change initiatives in the past.
- The leadership training program added a course on engaging teams through change that was developed based on our methodology and co-facilitated by our team to hundreds of leaders.
- The centralized communication team was able to leverage our communication elements to help successfully launch their new company-wide intranet platform.

- Three of the largest leadership events in the company's history were developed and supported in part by our team. We brought change adoption elements into each of those events and many of their activities to ensure leaders would get the most out of the experiences and distribute consumable and relevant learnings to their teams.
- We hosted well-attended monthly virtual meetings to provide opportunities for senior leaders driving any strategic initiative to engage directly with physicians and employees.

The exceptional results achieved at HNH are largely because healthcare companies do not typically invest in skilled change adoption resources. More often in healthcare, when the daunting task of implementation of an EHR begins, supporting the change experience is allocated to healthcare implementation consultants or delegated to Informatics, Human Resources, or Communications staff. I believe most industries started out in similar fashion, adding change adoption tasks to these types of teams. They realized over time that there are highly specialized skills required to really help employees through an emotional change experience and to make changing faster and easier.

It appears healthcare is on the same trajectory, just behind other industries. That is not all bad news though. If your organization has tasked these other teams with change work, they are bound to learn something and you will likely get some partial benefit from their efforts. Also, the change adoption methodologies and tools have come a long way in 30 years, so leveraging this work now is a lot easier and more streamlined. I am heavily networked with our nation's leading change experts, and we are seeing growing demand for change services in healthcare, so I'm hopeful every organization will invest in the right talent for change work.

I shared this case study to assure you that when leaders realize they are making transformational changes, hiring experts to help navigate the experience and make it faster and easier for impacted groups is money well spent. But, you don't have to take just my word for it. The next chapter tells the story of Epic working with the Change Adoption Team at Healing Neighbors Healthcare. Not only were the change adoption results impressive for HNH, Epic also was greatly enriched by working with the HNH Change Adoption Team.

Call to action!
Have you ever experienced an EHR implementation?
Compare your story to the one described
above…Take note of your insights here:

Chapter 6

Integrating Change Adoption into the Epic Implementation Plan

Epic is one of the nation's leading electronic health record (EHR) vendors. It is estimated that hospitals that use its software hold medical records of 54% of patients in the United States.[3] Healing Neighbors Healthcare chose Epic's EHR system because of the functionality of the software, the data and reporting capabilities, their track record of implementation successes, and the experience, support, and partnership Epic provides to their customers.

EHR software vendors commonly provide a comprehensive plan of everything that needs to be done in order to successfully implement their system. These plans include key milestones, activities, staffing resources, time allocations, and more. They outline the essential requirements of all work to be done to build, test, install hardware, train people to use it, and deploy their new EHR system. One of Epic's strengths is that they focus on end user adoption, and their comprehensive plans include many activities, programs, staffing recommendations, and time allocations for the people side of change.

Epic provides some essential change and adoption activities and deliverables in their planning material and engages leaders on being accountable for the changes that come with an EHR implementation. At Healing Neighbors Healthcare (HNH), my change adoption team worked very closely with Epic to integrate the entire change methodology, deliverables, activities, and measurements into the overall Epic project plan.

Marc Movrich, the Epic Implementation Director for Healing Neighbors Healthcare (HNH), has worked with many customers and has seen different ways they focus on end user adoption. Some customers focus mainly on communication support, some leverage their informatics or training teams, and others rely on operational leaders and existing staff for adoption activities. It is common for organizations with a large-scale change like an EHR implementation to have challenges with adoption, since emotions are always high at go-lives and inevitably there are always users who need more support. The value of a change and adoption team comes in their abilities in psychology, listening, communication, and leadership behavior. They are skilled in the emotional management of change, creating a positive, collaborative go-live experience, and minimizing the disruption that large-scale changes create.

When HNH decided to invest in a change and adoption team, Marc supported the idea and hoped he would also see firsthand what an expert change team would do to help guide leaders, physicians, and employees through a change of this magnitude. Marc had not worked with many change adoption professionals on previous EHR implementations, so this was a bird's eye view of our expertise applied to their methods.

As soon as I was on the ground, Marc welcomed me openly to the Epic Project Leadership Team. He carefully reviewed the change and communication activities that were already included in Epic's comprehensive implementation plan and welcomed the many more deliverables and activities I added for the change adoption effort. My communication plan contained more than 200 communication activities when we started. Approximately 250 were actually produced during the lifecycle of the project. For the change readiness activities, the Epic plan had key deliverables outlined, and I added more than 20 adoption measurements to ensure we were measuring and reporting people's readiness and adoption of the change.

During the time that Marc and I worked together, the benefits of our integrated efforts could not be overstated. Some highlights include the following:

■ HNH experienced faster and more successful implementations than any from its history.

- Epic staff supporting the go-lives gave praise for the positive attitudes they witnessed among operational staff and the project team.
- At the time, Epic typically planned for Command Centers to be in place for 2–4 weeks. HNH solved problems faster, friendlier, and with more collaboration than was expected, which allowed for Command Centers to close in less than 2 weeks!
- Super user support was also reduced more than a week early in most units in all locations at both go-lives.
- The change adoption team measured the attitudes of employees during the implementation, which was reported and addressed daily.
- More than 50 leaders who had previous experience with technology implementations graciously acknowledged my change adoption team for our contributions toward positive attitudes, readiness for change, and enhanced collaboration during go-live experiences.
- Closing the Command Centers early and reducing the contracted super user support saved HNH tens of thousands of dollars, and that savings was a direct result of people's preparation and attitudes during this transformation!

Prior to go-live, Marc and I were also able to collaborate on an "Executive Education Series," where we helped leaders get their heads around the key activities of the Epic project and what they needed to know. We presented vital information and provided targeted communication elements to help them cascade information so everyone knew what changes were coming, why they were important, and what role they needed to perform in the implementation.

These educational sessions helped support executives through their own change journey by providing them timely and consumable information and demonstrating the value of why they needed to know it. These sessions helped them be more confident and articulate about the changes and set them up for success with their teams when they disseminated our simple handouts to explain the concepts.

In line with preparing leaders, Marc and I also expanded Epic's standard "Leader Readiness Programs" for HNH. Epic had developed programs for hospital clinical leaders and revenue cycle leaders. My change adoption team modified and created additional leadership readiness programs for the remaining groups: clinics, labs, and physicians. The most impressive outcome of these Five Readiness Programs was the collaboration among all the operational leaders that were in the programs. Service Line leaders from each service and each location were able to meet, learn, and hear each other's stories. They learned about common challenges and innovative solutions from their peers. They experienced together the compromise of standardizing work processes, and they formed relationships. This increased the leadership change capability of all of HNH, beyond each leader's hospital, clinic, or department. These programs also measured leader readiness for change several times leading up to implementation and provided direct feedback loops to the team. If the leaders had questions or were not ready for change, we were able to address them immediately and get support activated.

More and more EHR implementations are now realizing the value and benefit of having a dedicated change adoption team and are asking about how to stand them up, what they do, and how they integrate with implementation project teams. Given our record of success, much of the work Marc and I did together enhanced Epic's comprehensive implementation plans with more change adoption activities, deliverables, and measurements.

Marc also asked me to meet with a few of their other clients to discuss our collaborative approach to change, communication, and employee adoption. As I said earlier, we are starting to see growing demand for change adoption support on EHR implementations, and these clients asked all the right questions. We typically shared an overview of our methodology and plans, and previewed some deliverables. While Epic remains a software company, they also recognize the importance of the people side of change and the value of having change adoption professionals integrated with an Epic implementation.

In summary, Epic knows what it takes to successfully implement their software and they understand the psychological journey leaders, physicians, and employees experience during a change of this magnitude. Over the past few years, they have collaborated with change adoption teams at various clients and have expanded their comprehensive plans to include more change and communication activities, milestones, and deliverables. Most importantly, they have seen firsthand the difference it makes and the value that can be achieved by having skilled change adoption professionals focusing on making leaders, physicians, and employees' emotional change experience as minimally disruptive as possible.

Did these stories of successful change adoption resonate? Do your vendors understand and value the people side of change like Epic? I hope you are thinking about what opportunities you may have at your organization to support the people side of the change.

Inspired by something you read?
Tweet about it **@DrKeelyK** or **#ChangeRxBook**

III

EXECUTIVES DRIVING CHANGE

Overview: This section provides executives with some critical insights about leading a large-scale change initiative and decision-making tools that help realize the required change support effort. Advice is given about sponsorship roles, and a case study about an exceptional executive sponsor is highlighted. The section ends with an Executive Sponsor Change Toolkit, which is a collection of three essential tools for scoping and leading any change initiative.

Your Prescription for Leading Change: Here are some immediate steps you can take to adopt the ideas in this section.

- Which of the duties described do you want to improve or increase next time you're leading a change initiative?— Story Teller, Super Hero, or Spark of Energy?
- Consider mocking up a Change Heat Map for the next 12 months. Does seeing all the change initiatives on a map inform your thinking about how your organization is resourced to support the changes or your employees' capacity to adopt them?

Chapter 7

Three Types of Leaders

Let's start with the premise that all leaders are involved and accountable for changes that are impacting their employees. Whether it's a small change or a big one, the leader is perceived as part of the change and is held accountable to ensure the change is adopted. Chances are, you have been a leader during a time when change was demanded of your people. In one way or another you were seen as a change leader by the people that work for you.

Your actions, attitudes, and words directly influenced how easy or hard the change was for your employees. Even if you did not make any decisions about what the change was or how it was implemented, your role as a leader contributed to the success or struggle your employees experienced in adopting the change. We follow our leaders implicitly, whether they are active or passive in their role.

So, if you are a leader and changes are happening, you are a change leader. Knowing the skills that are required to lead a change and sharpening these skills is essential for the successful adoption of your team. Leading change requires a person to have courage, abundantly communicate and listen, as well as to foster a safe and supportive environment for taking risks and learning. Even better, if you can lead passionately and inspire your team to embrace the change, you can make adoption more successful for everyone.

Call to action!

I hope we have all been lucky enough to work with a leader that was truly inspirational. Think of a leader like that in your work life. Ask yourself these questions and jot down your thoughts:

– What do I remember most vividly about them?

– What did they do to make me feel so inspired or motivated?

– Does anybody feel inspired by me in a similar way?

– What opportunities can I leverage through a change initiative to be more inspirational?

There are three fundamental roles leaders play in any change initiative:

1. **Executive sponsors**—Senior level leader accountable for the success of the entire initiative. Helps create the business case for change and is the liaison between the board or executive team and the change initiative as it is being implemented. The executive sponsor sets the strategy that directs the rest of the initiative team.

2. **Operations leaders**—Leaders of units, departments, clinics, or facilities that will be impacted by the change initiative. These leaders are key stakeholders of the initiative and should be involved in the project while still being able to keep business as usual. Resourcing constraints or temporary staffing assignments for these roles is driven by the executive sponsor.

3. **Project team leaders**—Directors and managers of teams who will lead the project work required to implement the change initiative. These are often project-based roles or temporary assignments, and staffing decisions for these roles are driven by the executive sponsor.

The focus of the rest of this section is on Executive Sponsors. If you are an Operational Leader or Project Team Leader, my best advice and tools for you are in Section 4: Leaders and People on Projects Making Change. The chapters that follow here are insights, skills, and tools that executives need to understand their role in leading change and to help scope change adoption needs for any transformational change initiative.

Chapter 8

The Best Advice for Executive Sponsors

Most large-scale changes are driven by business need, strategic initiative, competition in the market, and budget requirements. They involve executives, board meetings, business plans and proposals, and a lot of hard work done by a small group of leaders. This small group of leaders usually takes the initial idea and gets into the details to build a business plan and the budget forecasting. They have to learn a lot about the change itself, most of the moving parts, the vendors involved, any other external dependencies to determine costs and benefits. After that, they facilitate all the meetings to get approval and funding for the change initiative. From this small group arises the executive sponsor, who will lead and oversee the entire change initiative to its successful implementation. The executive sponsor is accountable for the whole change initiative, and this role can make or break a career. If you get an opportunity to serve as an executive sponsor, take it! The risk is great, but if you surround yourself with a team of competent people and support them tirelessly, the reward can be immeasurable. I have worked with many executive sponsors over the years and if you find yourself in this role or are considering one in the future, I have some helpful advice for you.

Executive sponsors are the name and face of a change initiative, which means power and risk. They have power and influence over the entire initiative, and they also have everyone who is impacted by the change initiative looking to them for answers and making judgments. If you believe in the change initiative and mobilize a team you can trust to get the work done, any sponsor can handle the power and the risk.

An executive sponsor has three very important roles and should focus on mastering the skills required to perform each of them. These critical roles are Story Teller, Super Hero and Spark of Energy. Executive Sponsor Duties describes them in more detail below.

Executive Sponsor Duties

Role	Description	Skills
Story teller	In this role, the sponsor needs to know a lot about the details of the change initiative and be able to talk about it at the right level for any audience. They need to be able to converse with board members about the value and importance of the change, and to the CIO about the technology team requirements, and also just as easily to operational staff about how they will be supported through this change.	• Communication • Self-awareness • Extroversion • Follow through • Confidence builder

Role	Description	Skills
Super hero	In this role, the sponsor will frequently save the day for the initiative. They can expect to make tough decisions, use their experience or connections to help remove barriers that will come up, or by bringing the right parties together to solve complex issues or close gaps that are discovered.	• Trust building • Conflict resolution • Empowering others • Collaborative
Spark of energy	In this role, the sponsor will ignite people around the change. They will focus on positives, share success stories, and celebrate milestone achievements. The sponsor will also keep conversations and momentum going as much as they can to help support the change initiative.	• Positivity • Gratitude • Motivating • Consistent

Like all executive leaders know, it takes the work of many hands to achieve any success. Leading a change initiative is the work of the executive sponsor's hands. The duties above are critical and should be considered carefully when naming a sponsor.

Change adoption professionals are essential partners for the executive sponsor and are very helpful in developing these skills and keeping these duties highlighted in the work of the sponsor. They can help the sponsor craft their stories and create opportunities for them to build momentum around the change, and can be a good feed-back filter. Change adoption professionals are direct chan-nels to all leaders, middle management, physicians, and employees so they have a good understanding of the pulse of an organization or how people think and feel about the things they hear from executives.

Change adoption professionals are also fiercely loyal to the sponsor, since that person is the key spokesperson for the change initiative. They have a vested interest in ensur-ing the sponsor does his or her duties exceptionally well, since that helps everyone to successfully adopt the changes that are coming. If you're leading a change initiative that is struggling to gain momentum or is unpopular, a change adoption professional can also help improve its receptivity or motivate a sponsor who might feel stuck leading one of these types of initiatives.

Call to action!
Reflect on your own experience as an Executive Sponsor.
Give yourself a score between 1 and 5 on your last
performance of each of the three roles:
- Story Teller
- Super Hero
- Spark of Energy

Chapter 9

Success Story:
An Exceptional
Executive Sponsor

Successful adoption is the goal of every large-scale change initiative. Adopting a change initiative includes deployment of a new software package or implementing a new process, but is broader. Adoption means employees are successfully operating in the desired new way that was defined in the business proposal when the change was envisioned.

Executive sponsors are accountable to the definition of success as it is outlined in the business case. Dr. Steve Gordon, MD, served as the executive sponsor for the Healing Neighbors Healthcare EHR implementation (see Chapter 5 for details). I have worked with many extraordinary executive sponsors throughout my career and want to highlight Dr. Gordon's talents for being a great Storyteller, Superhero and Spark of Energy to bring to life what this work really looks like for an executive sponsor.

For Dr. Gordon, physicians and employees were the primary focus and their change experience was paramount. Successful adoption meant that all physicians and employees were supported through their transformational change. Minimal disruption, change support, and readiness for the implementation were critical to the success for physicians and employees, so investing in a change adoption team was a reasonable investment. Epic and other vendors do not require a change adoption team, but they do recommend organizations have them to help with any implementation. Dr. Gordon knew the change adoption team would bring their unique set of skills, experience, change tools, and techniques to support employees' psychological experiences through the implementation.

The executive sponsor of any implementation must be visible, transparent, and engaged in the change effort constantly. Dr. Gordon created a monthly Virtual Open Forum, where physicians and employees from any corner of the health system could call in and hear updates about strategic initiatives, including the Epic EHR implementation, and ask leaders questions about anything. This openness and transparency helped build trust and understanding of changes and strategic direction. Additionally, Dr. Gordon helped create strong partnerships and collaboration among the corporate functions that influence or support changes in operations: communications, training, health informatics, Lean process improvement, and change adoption. He also knew the importance of having a change adoption team that had insight and input into the senior executive team, and he worked to ensure they knew the rest of the strategic landscape and changes that were being made outside of the EHR implementation. This was a new way of operating at Healing Neighbors Healthcare and allowed the change adoption team to help strategic decision making include the people side of change and consider the risks for adopting changes.

Beyond building transparency, partnerships, and strategic collaboration, Dr. Gordon also led with his presence. Showing up and listening was a core tenet of his sponsorship. Helping other leaders to engage and lead their departments and hospitals through this project was his key mission. Dr. Gordon would remove barriers for leaders by giving them guidance and information they needed to lead this change. He also would visit facilities when invited to help convey key messages or confidence and support of the Epic EHR implementation.

All in all, being an executive sponsor of a change initiative is mostly about helping others to have confidence in the change (Storyteller), walking the talk (Superhero), and believing in the change (Spark of Energy). It's about removing barriers for the project team to have success and about supporting other leaders in shepherding their employees through the change experience. Leaders often rise to the occasion without much support, but are always better off leveraging the help of change adoption professionals. This support can help with messaging and delivery, and most of all, creating transparency and support for frontline employees.

It turns out, even a story telling, super hero who is a spark of energy can benefit immensely from the support of change adoption professionals. At HNH, Dr. Gordon and I were strong partners. He intentionally sought my advice and perspective about our EHR implementation, as well as other strategic initiatives being discussed among the senior executive team. Dr. Gordon and I worked hard to be transparent and provide consumable, relevant information to leaders, physicians, and employees. We also created opportunities to speak and present at dozens of meetings so that almost every leader in every location had multiple chances of hearing our important messages. This effort paid off and we were rewarded with engaged leaders, awareness, and support for the initiative and in the end, faster adoption because of the investments everyone made before implementation.

Communication and engagement activities are the pillars of most change adoption work, and along with those efforts, we measure the value, effectiveness, and motivation those interactions provide. We measure people's feelings, behaviors, and attitudes toward the change experience, and in order to do that, we must develop trust.

If you are an executive sponsor, you are judged by many at each and every engagement. It is helpful actually to know how those efforts are received, and your change adoption professional can help you adjust or give you more support if needed. At HNH, we conducted more than 25 adoption measurements, and the responses on all of them were overwhelmingly positive. Of course we had a few negative responses, but those gave us the opportunity to have another conversation, grow relationships with our employees, and reinforce our messages in other venues. Again, it's invaluable to have a change adoption professional who can measure your impact on people, distill results into consumable reports, and help create opportunities for increasing adoption of your change initiative.

Remembering that an executive sponsor's key roles are Story Teller, Super Hero, and Spark of Energy, there are a few tools that are invaluable to this work. The next chapter will highlight my Executive Sponsor Change Toolkit, a collection of essential tools that support this role.

Call to action!
Starting to think you might need some change adoption support? Find Dr. Keely Killpack on LinkedIn to connect to the global network of change professionals!

Chapter 10

Executive Tools for Assessing Risk and Magnitude of Change

When a business goes through a transformation and the executive sponsor becomes the face of those changes, there are a few tools that can help you lead with your best foot forward. The Executive Sponsor Change Toolkit contains three essential tools for scoping and leading any change initiative. These tools are consulting industry standards, so they should be familiar. They are simplified and consumable versions and have been successful in helping others in scoping and articulating their change initiatives. It's important to start every change initiative in the best possible light, and these three tools can illustrate what resourcing is needed to ensure successful adoption of your change initiative (Table 10.1).

Table 10.1 Executive Sponsor Change Toolkit

	Tool	Description
1	**3-Legged stool**	Tool used to illustrate the scope of change in three common areas: people, process, and technology. Questions help drive answers and the tool can be used in any initial discussion of the change.
2	**Change risk quick query**	Survey tool used to scope the complexity of the people side of the change. Questions help determine change resource needs and change readiness of the organization at the beginning.
3	**Change heat map**	Planning tool to inform leaders of the competitive landscape surrounding the change initiative.

Note: Executive Sponsor Change Toolkit is available in full color download at http://www.ChangeRxBook.com.

1. **The 3-Legged Stool Tool** helps you assess and articulate the scope of changes in three common areas. These common areas are listed below and are frequently expressed as the 3-legged stool:
   - **People**—the attitude and aptitude of the employees performing the work tasks; their desire to want to do something a different way and their ability to learn and perform
   - **Processes**—the workflow or list of tasks and activities each job role performs
   - **Technology**—the devices, software, reports, or elimination of a manual task to an electronic one to perform the tasks of the job

   Any time you are talking about a transformational change, it is critical to realize the impacts in each of these three areas for every job role and employee you are expecting to change. Using a simple framework like this can help clarify what changes are coming and how they fit together for any job or employee. The stool also helps you realize what kind of support you need for the change.

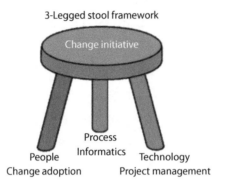

3-Legged stool framework

- **If you are changing people**—Change adoption support will help you support their attitudes and emotions surrounding the change (this makes adoption faster and easier).
- **If you are changing work processes**—Informatics support will help identify changes to process and support leaders and training to mirror the desired processes (knowing exactly what is changing for each job type and translating that for leaders, physicians, employees, and trainers).
- **If you are changing technology**—Project or program management support will keep the work on schedule and keep all the complexities together (tracking building, testing, interfacing, new hardware, and deploying technology).

The 3-Legged Stool Tool helps you scope your resource needs at a high level and share information with others about the complexity of the transformational change based on each leg of the stool. This is important if you are a person who will have to forecast budget for change adoption, informatics, or project management resources. The **3-Legged Stool Tool Template** provides questions and strategic thinking tips to help determine scope, build the stool image, and articulate the change.

Once you have the dimensions of the transformation identified, you need to know how much change will be required for employees or impacted groups (physicians, specific departments, vendor partners, etc.). Assessing the people side of the change in a little more focused way will help identify the complexity and determine how much change adoption support should be allocated to the effort.

2. **The Change Risk Quick Query** is a brief survey tool that helps identify complexity of the change and the recommended change support for getting impacted groups to successfully adopt changes quickly. This survey tool has 10 straightforward questions that measure the scope of change, mechanisms available to support the change experience, and the readiness of the organization to adopt a change. Anyone who has worked on the business case for the change initiative should be able to answer the questions and the executive sponsor benefits the most from knowing the responses. Once

you have the answers, it generates a scorecard with recommended change resourcing and deliverables.

Change risk quick query Read each question, circle the best answer					
Change criteria		**Questions**	**Magnitude of change**		
			Low	Medium	High
Scope	1	Changes typically involve people, processes and/or technology. Which of these 3 areas is this change impacting? Will stakeholder groups need new knowledge, new behaviors and/or new tools to perform job function?	Limited changes	Several changes	Many changes
	2	How many other change initiatives will be implementing during the same time period or competing for resources and attention?	None	Some	Many
	3	Approximately how many stakeholder groups will be affected? (groups can be units, clinics, specialties, physicians, vendors, etc.)	Few 1 to 10	Some 10–20	Many 20+
	4	Approximately how many end users will need to adopt a new way of working? (end user is defined as an individual who will need new knowledge, skills, and/or behavior to adopt the change)	Few 1 to 500	Some 500–1000	Many 1000+
Support	5	Has the business proposal been approved for this change initiative? Has the approval and future vision been communicated to all executive and senior leaders?	Yes and well received	Mostly	Limited commitment
	6	Are actions of senior leaders and their communications consistent with supporting the proposed change initiative? (walk the talk)	Consistent agreement	Some agreement	Little agreement
	7	Has a compelling case for change been articulated to impacted stakeholder groups? Do they understand the implications and business value for the change initiative?	Extensive understanding	Some understanding	Little understanding
Readiness	8	What is the organization's track record of change initiatives? What feelings will these stakeholders have about changes from the past?	Positive	Neutral	Negative
	9	To what extent are internal resources available to support the change initiative? (HR, marketing, communicationas, training, etc.)	All resources are engaged and will be leveraged	Some resources exist and can be leveraged	Little to no resources are available
	10	Does the organization utilize effective formal and informal communication methods? How easily can those methods be leveraged for the change initiative?	Yes or easy to leverage	Somewhat utilized or could be leveraged	Not consistently or hard to leverage

3. **The Change Heat Map** is the last of the tools in the Executive Sponsor Change Toolkit. The Change Heat Map is just what it sounds like: a map that shows hotspots for change. The Change Heat Map assumes that while this change initiative you are leading is going on, other change initiatives will also be occurring. It requires information gathering and collaboration from many to build the map, but it is absolutely

invaluable to determining timing and successful adoption. If you have a change adoption professional, they usually create this and keep it current as time goes on. If not, the executive sponsor takes the first pass at this and should try to find an owner to keep it up to date.

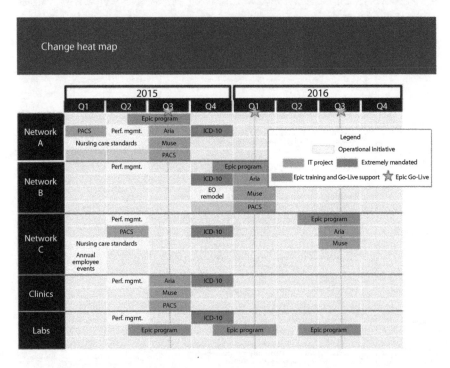

In the sample shown here, you can see that in 2015, Network A had several changes going on before the Epic Program, whereas Network B had very few competing initiatives before the Epic Program.

The Change Heat Map is most valuable because it shows you the competitive landscape of your change initiative to all the other activities that are planned. It gives you and your peers (all executives) a snapshot view of the changes they are asking people across the organization to adopt. It can show which groups or which times of the year are saturated with change or starved for innovation. This insight and connection for executive leadership is critical for seeing changes and anticipating gaps in support. Also, changes that may happen over multiyear periods or through multiple budget cycles are kept more transparent when they are seen on a Change Heat Map.

These three tools are designed to help any executive sponsor lead a change initiative and begin the change experience with their best foot forward. These tools also help decision making around investing in resources (like change adoption professionals, informatics support, and project management) and implementation timelines. Once these decisions are made, planning begins and the change adoption work of many is initiated. Pop icon Eddie Veder said it best, "Hold on! Hold on, friend," when reflecting about his change journey in the rock band Pearl Jam.[4]

Inspired by something you read?
Tweet about it **@DrKeelyK** or **#ChangeRxBook**

IV

LEADERS AND PEOPLE ON PROJECTS MAKING CHANGE

Overview: This section discusses five types of people who are typically involved in making change happen and some specific change needs for each of them. The challenging role of operational leaders during change is detailed, along with some best practices for leading change in that role. The influence project teams have in the change process is covered, and the body of change work is defined. Lastly, a Change Essentials Toolkit provides the basics for any change initiative to increase adoption.

Your Prescription for Leading Change: Here are some immediate steps you can take to adopt the ideas in this section.

- If you are involved in a change initiative right now, take a minute to answer the following:
  - **Change Diagnostics**—Did we figure out how big of a change this will be? Did we share that info with our stakeholders? What percent of them really have a good idea?
  - **Communications**—Do we have a plan for communicating? Do we publish communications that target specifically what the stakeholders care about?
  - **Engagements**—Do we engage our stakeholders? How often? Who—leaders, physicians, employees?
  - **Adoption**—Do we measure if those engagements are valuable and are helping stakeholders get ready to change? Do we share the results of the measures?
- If you work with consultants, take a moment to reflect on anything they have said or done beyond the scope of their service to you. Send them a quick email right now, expressing your gratitude for the advice or insights they have provided.

Chapter 11

Five Types of People Making Change

Despite being written by an organizational psychologist, this chapter is not about personality types! I'd like to discuss the different role types of people who typically make changes happen in an organization.

In my dozen years of change adoption experience, I commonly see the following types of people involved in making changes happen in any organization:

- Senior/executive leaders
- Operational leaders
- Service departments
- Project teams
- Consultants on project teams

Senior/executive leaders usually initiate projects, work on business case proposals, and become the "face of the project" if they are named as the sponsor. Everything I have to offer about this group is in the previous section. In Section 3:

Executives Driving Change, I address their role and duties, share some insights from an exceptional executive sponsor, and provide a few tools for them to assess change risk and determine the magnitude of change.

Operational leaders are usually the people who get double duty during a change initiative. They are responsible for keeping daily operations going as usual (their full-time job) as well as being asked to do several additional things to get their departments ready for a change to be implemented. Examples of operational leaders are ambulatory clinic managers, clinical service line directors, department managers, and medical staff office. Change-related activities for this group typically include planning, scheduling, budgeting, providing subject matter expertise, communicating, supporting their people more than normal, and much, much more. The next chapter is going to specifically discuss their change needs and expectations.

Service departments are those areas of an organization that serve others—human resources (HR), finance, sales and marketing, information technology (IT), research and regulation, etc. Oftentimes change initiatives are driven out of these departments to meet business requirements or in response to industry demand. Some familiar examples would include a new electronic health record (EHR) system, new talent management system and hiring process for managers, opening or closing of a facility, etc. Since many changes come from these departments, this can lead to a perception that the department is just pushing out changes and not really vested in operational needs. It is very important for change initiatives that are led by a service department to focus on their connection and service to the rest of operations. We will talk more about this in Chapter 13, "Advice for the Rest of the People Making Change."

Project teams are typically IT or HR teams that are pushing out a large-scale change. They regularly have employees from different parts of an organization participating in them (like a finance person to track the budget, a change or communication person to handle all the communicating, and a project manager to ensure all the work gets done, etc.). The important thing to keep in mind about project teams that are making change is that they need to have a sponsor that is recognizable and respected by the impacted stakeholders. They also need to focus on keeping their connection to the people the project is serving. Project teams often have consultants staffed on them as well. It is important to remember that if your project team is a mash-up of internal and external resources from all over the place, extra effort will need to be invested to ensure people work together cohesively and consistently communicate. I'm going to talk more about this in Chapter 13.

Consultants on project teams are vital, integral members of any change initiative. They bring unique, usually expert-level skills and talents. They help people within an organization stretch in new ways, and see things in a broader perspective. Consultants bring everything they know into their work at your organization and customize it to your needs, which is typically why they are more expensive than a full-time employee. They are also uniquely qualified to see gaps in current thinking or shortcomings, because they bring fresh, objective eyes and have seen multiple versions of whatever you are doing. The high points to be made about consultants are as follows:

- You should trust their expertise and their judgments (assume good intent and that they know what they are doing).
- They can help you succeed in a myriad of ways you might not be able to see initially.
- Integrating them with the rest of the team is the best way to get the most out of their service.
- If they have highly specialized skills that you don't think you will need after the change initiative … think again. It is almost always worth making sure your employees are tethered to your consultants and have the opportunity to learn from them.

Most types of people making changes in an organization should be covered in these categories. If you think I have left anyone out who doesn't fit in above, email me (drkeelyk@live.com)! For the change adoption professionals who work tirelessly to make changes happen in an organization, I have a separate section for you. Section 6: Change Adoption Profession details specifics of the change adoption role and provides basic tools for any practitioner.

Now that we have a common understanding of the five types of people who make changes happen in healthcare organizations, we are going to branch out and address the specifics. The next chapter is all about operational leaders and the chapter following that combines service departments, project teams, and consultants. The last chapter in this section showcases my "Change Essentials Toolkit," a collection of 11 tools for leaders and people who are making change.

Chapter 12

The Realities of Change for Operational Leaders

As I stated in the previous chapter, operational leaders are usually the people who get double duty during a change initiative. While this may feel like drawing the short straw, it is actually a reflection of the importance of this job. It's an honor and brings with it some power and responsibility.

Operational leaders' main role of daily operations means that you know how things are supposed to be done and how to motivate your staff to do those things. Both knowing how operations work and what makes your people tick is incredibly important for any change initiative. Since you are the point person for both things, you end up being the most qualified person to be involved in stakeholder decision making and readiness activities. You should expect to be involved and should be invested in making sure your voice is heard. Successful change initiatives involve key stakeholders like you, the people closest to the work, to help the change makers get it right.

At Healing Neighbors Healthcare (HNH), Epic recommended a Clinical Readiness Program concept, which we customized and expanded for our electronic health record (EHR) implementation. We formed Readiness Programs for each of our five stakeholder groups: Inpatient, Medical Group Clinics, Labs, Physicians, and Revenue Cycle. The Readiness Programs were essentially monthly meetings with key leaders in each group from all locations (for example, our Inpatient monthly meeting held 60 leaders, our Physician meetings held about 25, etc.). During these meetings, we would help operational leaders get ready for the implementation. This involved proposing our plans to them and then adjusting them based on their input. We also helped support them with registration, training, super users, resistance to change, and go-live preparation activities. It was a highly collaborative effort to get all the work done in ways that best fit the readiness groups (Inpatient, Clinics, Labs, etc.) and also trying to meet everyone's needs satisfactorily.

I share this story because it's difficult to ask operational leaders to do more. They are already spread pretty thin. Yet, they know so much and can really influence opinions and successful adoption of others. So, it's best to find a way to get their voices heard and their participation in your change initiative. At HNH, we spend a lot of time prepping and planning and vetting to make sure that every meeting was worth their time. We gave them consumable, simple handouts to share back in their departments and a checklist of things they needed to do before the next meeting. We constantly asked them what questions they had, what information they wanted, and helped them stay one step ahead of the change. In reaction to that, most of them were grateful and felt like the Readiness Programs were valuable and helpful and provided two-way communication between Operations and the EHR Project team. They also reported that they felt set up for success, like it was easy to share what they were learning in meetings and that they were ready when the implementation actually happened. This is another example of change adoption done well, when leaders report their perceived value of being involved and have collaborative, positive attitudes when large-scale implementations occur.

If you are an operational leader and you're being tasked with supporting a change initiative in these ways, I want you to know that your extra efforts are invaluable. Your success enables organization success, so take this responsibility seriously. If you think you or your unit/clinic/people need support to adopt a change, ask for it directly. Also, there are a few easy steps you can take to make change easier for your unit/clinic/people:

1. **Show support and confidence about the change initiative**—people respond to peoples' emotions and attitudes. We pick up emotions from those around us all the time.[5] If you act, feel, and think that this change will be helpful and successful, your people will also act, feel, and think that way.

2. **Share repeatedly the value of the change**—people need to hear messages about seven times before they remember them.[6] Having a concise, clear message about why this change makes sense and how we are going to successfully adopt it is critical. People on projects making changes should supply you with this "elevator pitch" so you can repeat it over and over again. If they don't, ask them for it.

3. **Keep communication open about the change**—people need to know there is a plan for getting to the finish line. They also need to have input and feel engaged in the process. An effective way to do both is to keep communication open and frequent about changes that lie ahead and the steps to take to get there.

4. **Increase your awareness of the change experience**—reflect on how you personally respond to change and learn how to support others through the change process. Change adoption professionals can help with this directly or you can Google and find tons of useful content.

5. **Be a compassionate leader**—provide time, support, and empathy for readiness activities, learning, practice, and the chaos of go-live transitions.

I admit, making a list of five action steps for you, the operational leader, is a lot easier than actually doing these things. But these are the basic actions of successful change leaders. If you can do these things, I promise you, the changes will be faster and easier than if you don't.

Call to action!
Reflect on a time you were part of a change in the past. Did you intentionally use any of these steps to help lead that change? Circle the ones you used before.

Chapter 14, "Change Essentials Toolkit," provides some samples and tools that help make these action steps a little bit easier. While they are designed predominately for people on projects who are making change, operational leaders can also benefit greatly from having these tools. Like HNH and in most large-scale change initiatives I have experienced, the project team provides operational leaders with many of the support tools you would need to adopt change successfully. That said, these tools work for smaller changes that may not have a dedicated team or change adoption professional. As I have said before, anyone in a leadership position is part of the change experience for frontline employees.

Chapter 13

Advice for the Rest
of the People
Making Change

Most large-scale change transformations are complex in all directions. They impact a lot of people, often in different ways or degrees. They are highly technical or involve sophisticated processes. It's easy to get lost in all the details and for leaders, physicians, and employees to feel overwhelmed or unclear about the changes coming their way. Service departments, project teams, and consultants are responsible for executing many of the change initiatives that senior leaders approve.

Service departments like human resources (HR) or information technology (IT) and project management offices (PMO) are full of people who bring changes upon their organizations. They are also the departments that typically form project teams and are often the face of change because so many of their employees work on implementing change initiatives. Since so many changes come from these departments, employees being impacted by their projects can have the perception that they are just pushing out changes and not really invested in operational needs. These perceptions are common and completely avoidable with dedicated change adoption resources and engaging key stakeholders in project activities (to varying degrees). Involving end users of a software package in the business requirements process seems pretty straightforward, and yet we all know of a recent project or two that glossed over it.

Project teams also have some other challenges to consider if they want successful change adoption. If your project team is a mash-up of internal and external resources from all over, extra effort will need to be invested in establishing cohesive relationships within the team, and socializing the team members with the impacted stakeholder groups. If you are leading a project with this type of makeup, you need to have the leadership skills to develop the team and build trust among the members. You should also help the team to create engagement opportunities to interact with their stakeholders directly.

Also, projects are intense, rapid-paced, and full of experts. Picture for a minute complete strangers rushing into your department, talking about concepts that don't make sense and using acronyms that don't mean anything to you. Then they start asking you a bunch of questions about how you do your work and record everything you say ... scary! Project teams need to remember who they are (highly skilled experts on a short timeline to do amazing things) and proceed with compassion and focus on keeping connected to the stakeholders they are serving.

Some essential things project teams should do to increase change adoption are as follows:

1. Select project sponsors that are respected by the impacted stakeholder groups.
2. Show confidence and support for the change initiative; always be positive about the project.
3. Start off with a basic, elevator story about the changes coming that minimizes fear (what is it, why are we doing it, what value will it bring to the organization).
4. Consistently repeat the benefits of the change and reinforce the elevator story.
5. Build on the elevator story with relevant details as they are timely and appropriate.
6. Keep communication open and constant about anything related to the change.
7. Plan extra time in the project for stakeholder readiness activities (lots of questions, security access, learning/training, practice, and the chaos of go-live transitions).

These are relatively simple things to do but require communication skills and dedicated effort. If your project team is larger than 10 people and your project impacts more than 300 people, a dedicated change adoption professional would be a wise investment and could support the team with these essentials and so much more. Change adoption professionals provide change support predominantly in the key areas provided in Table 13.1.

Table 13.1   Change Adoption Scope

	Key Area	Description
1	**Diagnostics and alignment**	Activities and deliverables to scope the magnitude of change, allocate budget, and align the change initiative to the organization's strategic direction.
2	**Communications**	All change initiative related communication planning, design, development, delivery, and feedback processing. Open communication channel directly to project team.
3	**Leadership and engagement**	All leadership change skill development, leadership support for leading a change initiative, leadership readiness programs (design, development, and execution). Engagement planning, events, coordination, and materials for distribution. Go-live support activities for project and stakeholders.
4	**Adoption measurement**	Measurements, distribution, and reporting for readiness for change, effective change engagement, and go-live change adoption.

In each of these areas, we leverage our psychological science skills to help motivate and build momentum for change. We also read human behavior queues and expressions for signs of fear and resistance. We leverage best practice tools and techniques to measure human behavior and create communications and engagements to increase the speed and decrease the hardship of adopting change.

Not every change requires expert skills and tools though. Some projects just need the basic, change essentials listed on page 81. In Chapter 14, the Change Essentials Toolkit provides tools for any project to use to support change and increase adoption.

Call to action!
Tell your team or some coworkers about something you learned in this section. Whatever resonates strongly, pass it on!

Chapter 14

Change Essentials Toolkit

Throughout this section, I have shared some insights about different roles people have during a change initiative. I have provided some specific behaviors and recommended activities that help make change faster and easier. Having said all of this, I'm a change adoption professional and some of our best assets are the tools we have to help others articulate a change or act in ways that help people through the change experience. So, I have included a few tools to help you. I have put together the **Change Essentials Toolkit** to support anyone leading or participating in a project making change.

The Change Essentials Toolkit contains eight tools. Table 14.1 describes each one briefly. A breakout section is also given for each of the tools with samples and additional detail. The entire collection of tools in the Change Essentials Toolkit is available to download in full color, and tool templates include the samples seen here along with easy-to-follow instructions for creating your own. I consider these eight tools the absolute minimum a project should have to support a change initiative.

Table 14.1 Change Essentials Toolkit

	Tool	Description
1	**Project vision**	A short, compelling elevator speech about the change initiative, its importance, and benefits to the organization and employees.
2	**Stakeholder circle**	A visual way to identify each of the audiences impacted by the changes coming that helps groups know they are important and on your radar.
3	**Meeting invite**	A simple Outlook Calendar template that helps leaders and project teams **engage audiences** in change activities. You will be setting up a lot of meetings and asking people to take a lot of time out of their days to meet with you. It's important to engage them and express gratitude for their time and energy.
4	**Timeline— high level**	A simple, high level view of the timeline for the change initiative. It is used to kick off the change and again at multiple points to help context setting or to remind groups of where we are in the big picture.
5	**Timeline— mid level**	A little more specific view of the timeline for the change initiative. It provides a few more details for various audience groups, depending on their change experience. It helps to illustrate complexity and gives a bit clearer of a picture of what is going to happen along the way.
6	**Timeline— key activities**	A detailed view of the activities or events that audience groups will experience. It doesn't show all of the work plan details, but does detail work that anyone in operations should expect to participate in, hear about, or know about.

(Continued)

Table 14.1 (Continued)   Change Essentials Toolkit

	Tool	Description
7	**Milestone tracker**	The most detailed view of all the readiness activities and milestone that involves operations. It lists everything operational leaders should keep track of, care about, or need to know. It helps leaders see the time and effort they will need to dedicate to this change and owners of activities.
8	**Milestone calendar**	This is the same detail as the Milestone Tracker, just shown in calendar format instead of listing activities by month. It is very helpful for posting on an office or break room wall to keep track of all the activities going on to get ready for a change implementation.

Note: Change Essentials Toolkit is available in full color download at http://www.ChangeRxBook.com.

14.1 TOOL #1 Project Vision

The **Project Vision** is a short, compelling elevator speech about the change initiative, its importance, and benefits to the organization and employees. Typically, the Project Sponsor or other Project Leadership of the change initiative will develop this project vision statement. They are created during the business planning for the change initiative and should be used broadly to ensure all employees in the company know what is coming, why we are doing it, and what benefits we expect from the effort. Create this or ask for it as soon as you are aware of the change initiative and keep it handy. It will be your starting point for conversations to come with all of your stakeholders or employees.

14.2 SAMPLE #1 Project Vision

This sample **Project Vision** statement from Healing Neighbors Healthcare (HNH) shown below was used in all communication mediums for months. Everywhere we were talking about our project, we started with the vision statement. This meant posters, flyers, meetings, emails, presentations, leader resources, and our project website all had the project vision:

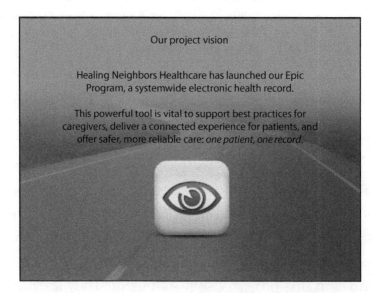

14.3 TOOL #2 Stakeholder Circle

The **Stakeholder Circle** is a visual way to identify each of the audiences impacted by the changes coming that helps groups know they are important and on your radar. The main utility of this circle is to show audiences that they are included in the change initiative. It also helps demonstrate your knowledge of each corner of the organization, as well as the broader landscape.

14.4 SAMPLE #2 Stakeholder Circle

This sample **Stakeholder Circle** shown below was used at HNH in all initial engagement meetings for months. Everywhere we were presenting information about our change initiative, we used this circle to show the audience they were going to be changing. We also used it when we initiated our five Readiness Programs to level set with any operational leaders that may have missed the initial meetings.

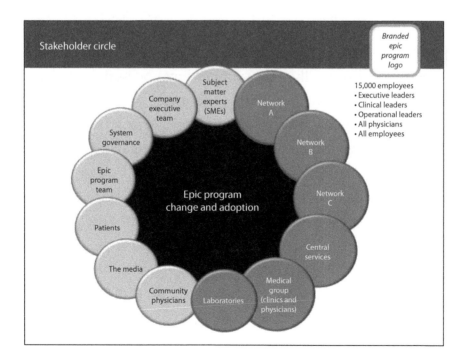

14.5 TOOL #3 Meeting Invite

The **Meeting Invite** is a simple Outlook Calendar template. It helps set the tone of engagement and appreciation even before you meet people. It helps leaders and project team members engage audiences in change activities. You will be setting up a lot of meetings and asking people to take time out of their days to meet with you. It's important to put your best foot forward and express gratitude for their time and energy. Believe it or not, this approach to meeting invitations is, by far, the most influential tool in this toolkit.

14.6 SAMPLE #3 Meeting Invite

The sample **Meeting Invite** shown below illustrates how just a few words and formatting make all the difference in attendance, especially if you do not have personal relationships with invitees. The "Before" image, on the left, was the standard meeting invitation at HNH. When our change adoption team became more involved in engagement planning, we developed the "After" version for all project team events. We received positive feedback from many invitees saying they appreciated being invited and given the agenda ahead of time so they knew what to expect. It seems like common sense as you view these side by side, but look at your own calendar for a minute and take notice of which meeting organizers take the time to make you feel invited, welcome, and vital.

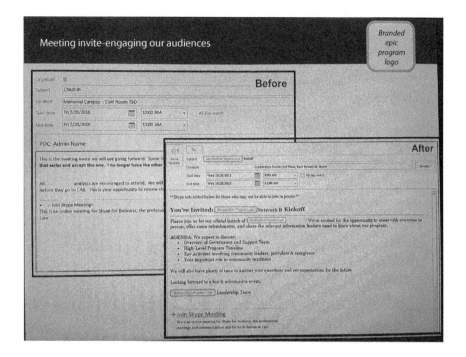

14.7 TOOL #4 Timeline—High Level

The **Timeline—High Level** is a simple, high level view of the timeline for the change initiative. It is used to kick off the change and at many points along the way to remind groups of where we are in the big picture or to onboard new people to the change initiative.

14.8 SAMPLE #4 Timeline—High Level

The sample **Timeline—High Level** shown below illustrates the entire change initiative in a half page! It shows the five large IT project implementations during a 2-year window. This timeline was useful because almost every employee at HNH was impacted by these changes and it is a quick easy view of when they were coming.

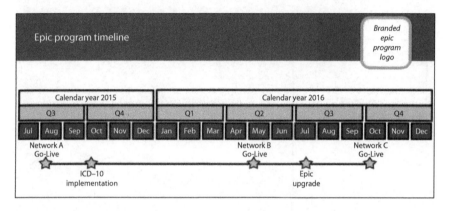

14.9 TOOL #5 Timeline—Mid Level

The **Timeline—Mid Level** provides a few more details for various audience groups, depending on their change experience. It helps to illustrate complexity and gives a clearer picture of the whole change initiative and what is going to happen along the way.

14.10 SAMPLE #5 Timeline—Mid Level

The sample **Timeline—Mid Level** shown below illustrates the entire change initiative for each stakeholder group. Specifically, employees could see the high level activities they would be experiencing. They could also see the work being done in other networks and how all the pieces fit together in the organization. This view of the timeline was used constantly to help articulate where everybody was in their change experience, as well as when resourcing, budget, and timing discussions took place. This view doesn't tell a reader everything, but it tells them enough to know how they fit into the big picture and what each piece looks like.

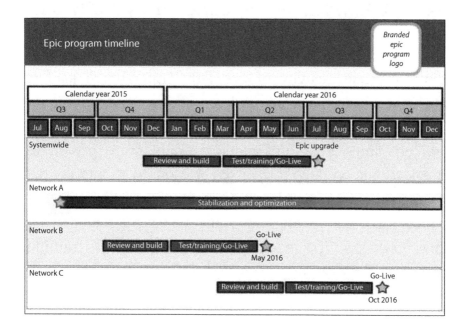

14.11 TOOL #6 Timeline—Key Activities

The **Timeline—Key Activities** is a detailed view of the activities or events that audience groups will experience.

It does not show all of the work plan details, but does detail work that anyone in operations should expect to participate in, hear about, or know about. It is an essential tool during any large-scale change. It helps all leaders know how to lead a change, the key activities they need to perform and when, as well as keeps everyone consistent across any size organization.

14.12 SAMPLE #6 Timeline—Key Activities

The sample **Timeline—Key Activities** shown below illustrates each activity or event that operational leaders are expected to know about, learn about, or participate in. This timeline was widely distributed in all online, written, printed, and verbal presentations. Many were posted in break rooms on large format paper, along with a table that briefly described each box on the timeline. The color version is more compelling, but you can see that activities are color coded, so if a reader wants to know all the training activities, they can see them at the top and know what they are and when they happen.

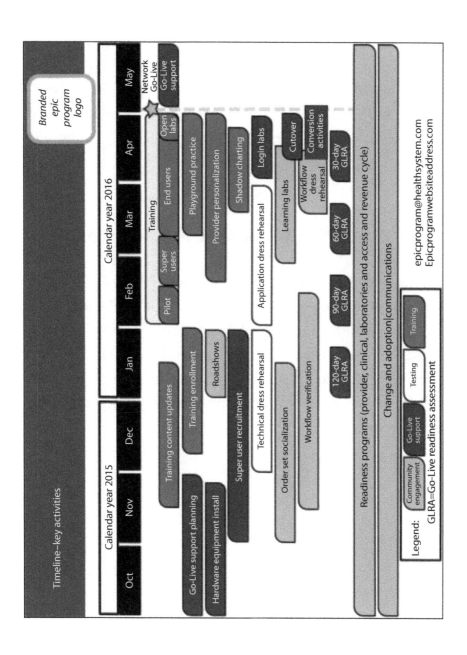

14.13 TOOL #7 Milestone Tracker

The Milestone Tracker is the most detailed view of a change initiative and shows all the readiness activities and milestones that involve operations. It lists everything operational leaders should keep track of, care about, or need to know. It helps leaders see the time and effort they will need to dedicate to this change.

14.14 SAMPLE #7 Milestone Tracker

The sample **Milestone Tracker** shown below illustrates 1 month of readiness activities for our EHR implementation. This list provides a comprehensive look at every activity, including when, what, who, where, and why. Previous versions also included the owner or contact person for each milestone, which was very helpful getting inquiries to the right person.

Branded epic program logo

Milestone tracker

Legend: Testing | Training | Readiness | Go-Live planning and support

Month	Dates	Milestone	Objective	Networks impacted		
June	June 1, 22	Provider readiness meeting	Ongoing meeting of medical and operational leaders to plan and prepare for provider-specific *branded epic program* activities.	A	B	C
	June 2, 9, 16, 23, 30	Network adoption team meeting	Weekly meeting of network A operational and clinical leaders to discuss ongoing *branded epic program* activities.	A	B	C
	June 3	GLRA-60-day	Go-Live readiness assessment (GLRA) 60-days prior to go-live to review and determine any mitigations needed for network A.	A	B	C
	June 3, 17	Provider readiness meeting	Ongoing meeting of medical and operational leaders to plan and prepare for provider-specific *branded epic program* activities.	A	B	C
	June 4, 11, 18, 25	Lab readiness meeting	Ongoing meeting of network A lab and operational leaders to plan and prepare for lab-specific *branded epic program* activities.	A	B	C
	June 8	End-user training begins	Network A caregivers and providers begin completing their required end-user training. Training will be open June 8–July 27.	A	B	C
	June 10	Clinical readiness meeting	Clinical and operational leaders from all networks meet to discuss key *branded epic program* activities.	A	B	C
	June 11	Revenue cycle meeting	Operational and project team members meet to share information, monitor project progress, and establish risk mitigation plans.	A	B	C
	June 16	Medical exec. meeting	Monthly *branded epic program* update for medical executive committee members.	A	B	C
	June 18	Cutover dry run	Cutover dry run practice to prepare for transitioning workflows, data, charts and users from legacy system to *branded epic program*.	A	B	C

14.15 TOOL #8 Milestone Calendar

The Milestone Calendar contains much of the same detail as the Milestone Tracker, just shown in calendar format instead of a table listing each activity. It still provides the most detailed view of all the readiness activities and milestones that involve operations. This calendar view proved to be very helpful for posting on an office or break room wall to keep track of all the activities going on to get ready for the change implementation.

14.16 SAMPLE #8 Milestone Calendar

The sample **Milestone Calendar** shown below displays all of the activities from Tool #7 Milestone Tracker, just in calendar view instead of a table. It does not include the objectives for each activity; however, this calendar version accompanied the tracker version each time we distributed them. Prior versions also had our email address and web address on the bottom of each page, so if someone was looking at this calendar view and had questions, they could easily contact someone to get an answer.

Branded epic program logo

Milestone calendar

Legend: Testing · Training · Readiness · Go-Live planning and support

June

Sun	Mon	Tues	Wed	Thurs	Fri	Sat
	1 Provider readiness mtg.	2 Network adoption team mtg.	3 GLRA–60-day / Provider readiness mtg.	4 Lab readiness	5	6
7	8 End user training begins	9 Network adoption team mtg.	10 Clinical readiness mtg.	11 Revenue cycle mtg. / Lab readiness mtg.	12	13
14	15	16 Network adoption team mtg. / Medical exec. mtg.	17 Provider readiness mtg.	18 Cutover dry run / Lab readiness	19	20
21	22 Provider readiness mtg.	23 Medical exec. mtg.	24	25 Lab readiness	26	27
28	29	30 Network adoption team mtg.				

The eight tools showcased above in this **Change Essentials Toolkit** are the bare essentials for any change initiative. To make change faster and easier, you need to be able to tell the story of the change in a consumable way, that gives people the information they need, as they need it. They need to know the value of the change initiative and how it benefits them, so people can begin their adoption process right away. If you have change adoption support on your project, they would be the best at crafting these materials and keeping them current. They also have a lot more tools for adopting change and should be able to effectively use them anywhere. If you do not have dedicated, skilled change adoption support, anyone on a project can create these from scratch or get a jumpstart by downloading the full color toolkit (http://www.ChangeRxBook.com).

Call to action!
Starting to think you might need some change adoption support? Find Dr. Keely Killpack on LinkedIn to connect to the global network of change professionals!

V

PHYSICIAN SUPPORT THROUGH CHANGE

Overview: This section discusses the unique change needs of physicians and how to design a team to support them. It discusses the power and pressure that surround a physician as well as some important considerations related to burnout.

Your Prescription for Leading Change: Here are some immediate steps you can take to adopt the ideas in this section.

- Recall from earlier or identify a few of the change initiatives at your organization. Consider the percentage of physicians that are impacted by them and the percentage of physicians involved in each change initiative. If physician engagement is lacking, talk to a decision maker about it.

- Share key highlights of this chapter with your Chief of Staff or Medical Staff Officers. Maximize your effort of reading this section so it can influence your physician population.
- Create a quick one-page summary of information in this chapter that is relevant for your physicians. Ask your Medical Staff Office if you can present it at their next meeting.

Chapter 15

Dedicate Resources for Physician Change

It is common knowledge that physicians are a unique stake-holder group in healthcare. They have varying employment arrangements (employee, contracted, community, privileged at multiple locations, solely independent, etc.), and their change experience is also more complex than other groups because of the range of changes for each specialty. Depending on the physician's employment type, they may have to use several different EHR platforms, or the same one configured in different ways depending on where they practice. They are also somewhat leaderless. Although physicians do have extensive governance from peers and regulators, a typical service line director in a hospital or a clinic manager has much less authority or influence over their behavior or motivation to change it. Don't forget that physicians are almost always time constrained as well.

So, how do you get the attention of a group of people who are really smart and powerful, who have limited free time, and convince them to learn something new? How do you help them adopt the new behavior especially when it will slow them down in the beginning and then give them benefits they may not value yet? The short answer is that you recruit some of them to engage in the change initiative, you provide essential information in the most consumable ways, you create incentives for adoption, and you dedicate support resources to help them through their change process.

At Healing Neighbors Healthcare (HNH), there was a dedicated group of team members who supported the physician experience, from the initial planning for the EHR implementation until months after each location was on the new system and adopting new work processes. This Physician Support Team included the following:

■ **Chief Medical Information Officer (CMIO)**—an MD turned Administrative Physician, head of all people, process, and tech changes for physicians
■ **Physician Champions**—physicians in various specialties with EHR experience, who acted as subject matter experts, coaches, trainers, and super users, and led their physician peers and medical staff officers through the change journey

- **Health Informatics Physician Liaison**—document and standardize physician work processes by specialty, support training, and change adoption
- **Clinical Content and Decision Support Physician Liaison**—facilitate engagement and standardization of all clinical support content (order sets, flowsheets, etc.) by specialty
- **Change Adoption Provider Professional**—plan and track all physician group engagements, prepare and distribute communication and engagement materials for each physician group or event, measure influence, and track change adoption
- **Training Lead for Physician Curriculum**—design, develop, and deliver physician training courses for each specialty or physician type

The collaboration among this group, the support they provided, and the myriad of ways they were able to engage with physicians of all types were very effective leading up to and following the EHR implementation. They attended dozens of Medical Staff events, hosted open labs in private physician lounges to be conveniently available to doctors at any time, and did endless hours of rounding and one-on-one conversations with physicians about their change experience. An email digest was designed just for physicians, which distributed important, timely information just for them and created an open, personal communication channel to answer their questions.

This team was invested in physician engagement in order to help them in making big changes to their behavior, work processes, and technology.

Equally important was the fact that there was a lot of activity they needed to participate in to get ready for the new operating model. Figure 15.1 shows the key activities that each physician needed to experience.

This Physician Support Team also implemented a Physician Readiness Program. The program was led by the CMIO and the Champions and was a tool provided by Epic. Our Change Adoption Professional customized the program, structured and developed its content, and supported delivery of each session. The Physician Readiness Program essentially brought together a group of involved and revered physicians from varying practices at each location once or twice a month, depending on the demand. During

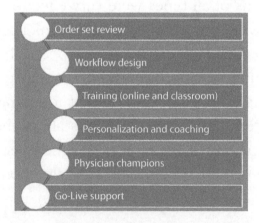

Figure 15.1 Key activities for physicians.

the meetings, the CMIO and the Physician Champion provided important information about the changes coming,
and the Change Adoption Professional ensured the materials were easily consumable and distributed to the members
to share with their colleagues in each practice. Many of
the key activities in the diagram above were addressed in
these meetings, and the physicians' attitudes and readiness
for change were also measured and published.

The biggest benefit of the Physician Readiness Program
was getting physicians from varying practices together to
hear, learn, and prepare for change. This helped everyone
get their questions answered, learn more, and realize their
colleagues have many of the same fears and frustrations.
It also helped prepare physicians for the implementation
experience and established relationships so everyone felt
more comfortable asking for help if they needed it.

The success of this Physician Support Team was impressive and exceeded everyone's expectations. Most notably
was the camaraderie and collaborative attitudes of the
Physician Readiness Program members, especially during
the implementation. Doctors helping doctors actively find
help when they needed it meant that all the preparation
was worth it! The quantitative results revealed more than
95% of all physicians attended and passed their training
courses before implementation, and within 6 weeks following it, more than 80% had personalized in some way (view
preferences, order sets, etc.). The EHR technology was also
implemented with fairly minor issues. In fact, the on-site
command center was shut down more than 1 week early,

and super user support was reduced after just 2 weeks of implementation in all locations. In other words, faster and easier adoption of new technology and processes than anyone expected or had planned!

Call to action!
Circle concepts in this chapter that you didn't know before and that you think would be valuable to share where you work.
Put a reminder on your calendar to tell a decision making leader about it before the week is over.

Despite all of the success with the HNH implementation, there are always a few hurdles to overcome and those that resist. In this case and likely in whatever changes you are making in your organization, sometimes there is risk to pushing people out of their comfort zone and for asking a group to do everything in a new and different way. This is especially true when the people are very smart, have power and control, and you are asking them to surrender some of it. Sometimes the request to change and adopt new behaviors and tools can be too much and can lead to physician burnout. I'd like to spend the next chapter addressing a little more deeply the emotional experience of change for physicians and some important elements related to physician burnout.

Chapter 16

Physician Burnout
Is Real

Physicians hold immense power and authority in healthcare—after all, they are the brains behind saving lives! They are in high demand and spread pretty thin most of the time. Being in a position of control and influence also comes with a lot of pressure and risk. Failure is not an option. Because physicians are expected to be super human (all knowing, all powerful, all healing), it can be more challenging to motivate them to change, especially if those changes minimize their power or add to an already overfull plate. If you are making changes that impact physicians, you need to be aware that the stakes are higher for this group to adopt and their change support needs are likely to be greater than other groups.

In any change initiative, some decisions or expectations are not going to be universally popular. That's completely normal and everyone should anticipate a negative reaction to a change at first, and some resistance throughout the change process. We know from neuroscience and psychology that most people resist change initially, and that applies to physicians like any other human being.[7] Be prepared to have some negative reception at the onset and move forward. I tell leaders that negative reception is a good thing, and when we hear it in the beginning, we know that people are starting their change experience. If it persists, leaders need to breathe deeply, put on their shield of courage, and just be transparent. Delaying decision making or not addressing resistance will only result in a loss of momentum and could jeopardize a leader's credibility. If continued communication and engagement doesn't get the resistors to come around, it is critical to find a change adoption professional quickly.

Physicians have some additional positional pressures that need to be considered by anyone supporting them through a large-scale change initiative. This is because change can contribute to burnout, which is defined as physical or mental collapse caused by overwork or stress.[8] Physicians have an increased risk of burnout anyway, and a recent study published by the Mayo Clinic claimed that 54% of US physicians suffer at least one symptom of burnout.[9] Burnout can lead to medical mistakes, depression, and even suicide. It has been known for ages that physicians have one of the highest suicide rates of any profession, and it is estimated that at least one physician takes his or her own life each day.[10] It's important to acknowledge this because change initiatives are short-term, intense burdens and if your audience is high risk for burnout, depression, and suicide, adding a large, difficult change to their workload needs to be carefully evaluated and vetted with your physician population before you get started.

Physician burnout is a condition we need to bring to light, learn more about, and react accordingly. At a minimum, the factors that contribute to burnout and results of burnout are listed below. Let's start the conversation:

1. **Factors that contribute to physician burnout**
   - Burdensome administrative tasks
   - Changes in the healthcare environment (i.e., technology, policy/regulation, etc.)
   - Loss of control/autonomy
   - Work/life balance
2. **Results of physician burnout**
   - Anxiety
   - Decreased productivity
   - Depression
   - Medical mistakes
   - Substance abuse
   - Suicide

Burnout is a serious concern and change initiatives can contribute to physician burnout, so we all need to get real about addressing it effectively. Engage physicians in a dialogue about burnout. These conversations are best privately and peer-to-peer, but even a healthcare administrator or change adoption professional could begin these conversations. Acknowledging this risk, what contributes to it, and what support is needed or available is the best first step. Here are some suggestions for support to minimize burnout:

3. **Ways to help minimize physician burnout:**
   - **Get it out in the open**—have open and honest dialogue about burnout. Create opportunities for physicians to engage in the subject and get help if they need it.
   - **Lighten the load**—reduce the number of meetings or create proxy process, reduce non-essential paperwork, automate payer letters or reminders.
   - **Promote wellness**—prioritize stress reduction, self-care, work/life balance.
   - **Educate on change experience**—articulate what to expect during times of change and what physicians need to do, address any loss of control concerns, address change resistance.
   - **Peer network**—help physicians connect with each other and have private conversations (coaching, counseling, ethicist, or a wellness group) if they are overwhelmed or struggling.
   - **Escalation point**—identify a physician or chief of staff who can be the contact person if a physician is in need. Prepare that person with the tools he or she needs to respond and inform physicians that there is a person there to help.

Dike Drummond, MD, is one of the leading experts on physician burnout. He has a book, a website, and more than 100 free powerful tools and tips available. The most helpful things I have seen can be found here: http://www .thehappymd.com.

When we stop to reflect, we realize physician attitudes and their well-being can largely influence the rest of the staff and the patient. Their attitude can set the tone for an entire hospital floor, a team of people assisting in a procedure, or a whole clinic. Their espoused support for a change initiative could help the rest of their staff adopt it easier. Their power and influence reach out far and wide and can impact everyone around them. Ensuring that physicians have what they need to successfully adopt whatever changes you are bringing to your organization should be a top priority. With so much at stake and arguably a lot to lose, I strongly recommend you engage a change adoption professional to help support your physician's change experience.

The risk of not assessing physician burnout can threaten patient care and influence unit/clinic morale. Don't wait another day to open the dialogue about the reality of physician burnout and ways your organization can help minimize it.

Inspired by something you read?
Tweet about it **@DrKeelyK** or **#ChangeRxBook**

VI

THE CHANGE ADOPTION PROFESSION

Overview: This section gives away all the industry secrets! Actually, it covers the type of people who do this work and the skills they have, a broad stroke of the leading Change Management theories, and finally, a toolkit full of more engaging and dynamic tools to help make change faster and easier.

Your Prescription for Leading Change: Here are some immediate steps you can take to adopt the ideas in this section.

■ If you have ever worked with a Change Adoption Professional in the past, reflect on their strengths. Write down all the ways they shine bright and compare your thoughts to the list of talents described in this section.

■ Think about your own industry or career niche. Can you list all the founding theories that your industry is built upon? Do you know experts in each theory? Spend a few minutes considering how you might describe the people and the theories that are the basis of the work in your field.

■ Identify the top 5 tools you use in your role that you think are the most effective. Consider sharing them with a handful of your peers next time the opportunity presents itself.

Chapter 17

Our People, Our Craft

Change adoption professionals at their core are usually:

- Compassionate and empathetic
- Team oriented with positive disposition
- Intuitive, psychological problem solvers
- Intentional communicators

We care about people and the hardship we know they will experience through change. We do countless things to make change *feel* better. For each change initiative we support, we work hard to establish relationships with 100s of people because they need to trust us in order to make change faster and easier. We all know that people typically react negatively to change at first, and a big part of our job is to absorb that initial negativity and help people move past it. Nobody would expose themselves to skepticism and negative emotional outbursts regularly unless they genuinely cared about people and wanted to help make their change experience *feel* better.

We often work alone, as an individual contributor on a project team or as a member of a change team but supporting a location by ourselves. Even though we are highly independent, we are usually thinking of ways to stay tethered to our own team, or to connect with our stakeholders that will be changing because of our project work. Most of our work involves interacting, so we are always engaging with groups of people and helping teams come together around the change initiative.

We are also fairly intuitive people. We have keen powers of observation, we are highly analytical, and many of us have psychology and neuroscience backgrounds too. We like to keep our eyes, ears, and sixth sense open to our stakeholders so we can best help them. We read people and analyze their emotions. We often track people's emotional journeys and coach leaders to behave in ways that directly respond to emotional reactions to change. Our attention and focus on how people feel and react can be intimidating to some, but I promise our intentions are genuine and we are putting all that we have to good use.

We are very intentional communicators and are often considered skilled public relations specialists and marketers. Our job is to help people adopt a new way of thinking and doing. We do this with simple and consumable communications, powerful presentations, action-orientation, and by spreading positive, confident attitudes that lead to success. We also try to infuse innovation and fun into our work, because a software demo is only as exciting as the costumes of the people clicking the mouse and talking about the screenshots, right? Like any skilled communicator, measuring our stakeholders is paramount. We are constantly asking, measuring, and reacting to the receptivity of our messages by our audience groups. Change adoption professionals use measurements to determine people's readiness or resistance to change and the effectiveness of our efforts to support people through the change experience.

Many of us come from communication and marketing backgrounds and both industries really strengthen each other. The psychological elements of the change work are intertwined in our communication and leadership engagements, which always require marketing and materials. When communication teams partner with change teams, both groups win big. The following story illustrates this perfectly.

At Healing Neighbors Healthcare (HNH), our electronic health record (EHR) implementation reached almost everyone, in varying ways, at varying times, and with varying levels of engagement. All of this complexity in the change experience meant that the communication effort was going to be vital, complicated, and very large. Communication is one of the main components of every change adoption methodology. It was important to collaborate with HNH's corporate communications department to ensure that we were being consistent with our messaging, tone, and branding standards. Our change adoption team had two dedicated communication members and the other eight change professionals also created communication elements. In total, we created, developed, and distributed more than 250 communication elements during the course of the EHR implementation. Our two dedicated communication team members could never have done all of that work by themselves, nor could the corporate communications department take on an additional 250 pieces of work without dedicating resources for the EHR implementation. This is important because it would have been easy to operate in a silo and just execute our communications without collaborating with our corporate partners. But that extra effort was more beneficial than anyone imagined, and our change adoption team success had far reaching benefits for our corporate communication department:

■ We created and implemented HNH's standard enterprise-wide communication plan. Everyone experienced how well it works, and now it can be leveraged for the next large-scale change initiative.
■ We helped integrate change adoption principles into the standard communication approach for other communication messaging. Our standard practice to include psychological and motivational messaging in our elements is now leveraged for other corporate communications.
■ We were able to add more reviewers, approvers, and content developers to the communication process. This reduced our cycle time significantly for each communication element.

- Our change adoption team also shared innovative communication elements, templates, and tools with the corporate communications team and with leaders in all locations.
- Our EHR communications (articles, events, handouts, website) also helped to launch HNH's intranet site that connected all locations to a single web platform of news and information. It turned out to be very effective to have a large-scale change to drive the interest of all employees to a new digital communication platform.
- The collaboration between the corporate communications department and our change team meant that our audience had a consistent, intentional experience every time they read or received a communication. This was invaluable when you consider how it increased trust and reduced skepticism about the changes coming, each and every time a communication is distributed.

Change adoption is a challenging and rewarding profession. As we master our skills and simplify our complex methodologies, we have so many opportunities to expand our reach and we are definitely branching out! There are a few of us in the agile software development space, working with startups and entrepreneurs as well as family-owned small businesses and everything in between. Our popularity in healthcare is also growing as this industry transforms and tries to keep competitive in the complexity of America's health.

If you are leading a change or executing one and you think you may need a change adoption professional, we are here to help! Change adoption professionals use psychology and business acumen to understand the people side of change and what tools work best to bring employees along their change journey. We have a global professional association (acmpglobal.org), certification courses in a few methodologies, and backgrounds in psychology and/ or organizational studies. There are thousands of practitioners who have worked in all corners of the business world. Many of us work as consultants, contracted to an organization for a large-scale transformation, and then released as these changes settle and stick. Others are internal employees, in dedicated change or transition business units, supporting all the changes and transformations an organization is generating. As a unit, we are better able to ensure minimal disruption to operations and a smooth transition for all employees, regardless of the change.

Call to action!
Does anything in this chapter surprise you? How closely does your perception of change adoption work match the way it is described in this chapter?

Chapter 18

Change Theory Mash-Up

Our talents and skills have been uncovered, but are you still asking yourself about our theories and methodologies? If you are curious about our history and methods, this chapter has answers.

The very first known efforts of measuring and managing changes in the workplace actually began in the industrial revolution (late 1700s–early 1800s) as Britain was moving manufacturing to factories and getting people to adopt the use of machinery instead of doing everything by hand.[11]

However, most experts say that change management as an industry officially grew out of the Elisabeth Kubler-Ross' five stages of grief back in 1969.[12] Even today, her change curve is one of our most recognizable tools (Chapter 19 talks more about that specifically).

It's worth mentioning that during the 1960s and 1970s, psychologists were also developing theories and doing research on changing behavior. In 1960 and for 30 years, Edwin Locke studied work motivation and behavior change through goal setting.[13,14] In 1977, Albert Bandura founded his social cognitive theory, which supported behavior change levers in the workplace based on social desirability.[15]

So, we've been studying, experimenting, and postulating about how to get employees to change how they work for a very, very long time. And the research and interest continues to this day. Recent studies in neuroscience and physiology are adding theories and methods to change science as well.

Aside from these greats and the emerging newcomers, there are a few theories and methodologies that have been around for the bulk of the last 30 years and are the "tried and true" methods of change management. Anyone who is a change adoption professional should be familiar with each of these methods in name and broad concept. For readers who are not expert, I'm going to provide the basic fundamentals of the most common theories in change practice. To avoid any bias, they will be in alphabetical order:

1. ADKAR™ by Prosci
2. AIM™ by IMA
3. Being First by Change Leaders
4. Bridges' Transition Model
5. CAP™ by GE
6. Kotter's 8 Step Model
7. The Standard for Change Management by ACMP
8. Your Organization

1. **ADKAR™ by Prosci**—In most circles, Prosci's ADKAR™ model is the most common methodology in the United States. It uses a three-phase approach: Preparing for Change, Managing Change, and Reinforcing Change. Each phase contains planning tools, deliverables, activities, and assessments. It's a comprehensive methodology and Prosci also leads research in our industry with industry benchmarks and leading edge measurement tools.[16]

2. **AIM™ by IMA**—Accelerating Implementation Methodology (AIM). Uses a three-phase approach: Plan, Implement, and Monitor, and in addition has a 10-step model. Each step contains planning tools, deliverables, activities, and assessments.[17]

3. **Being First™ by Change Leaders**—Uses a three-phase approach: Foundations, Design, and Implementation, and a nine-step process. Each step contains planning tools, deliverables, activities, and assessments.[18]

4. **Bridges' Transition Model**—Uses a three-stage approach: Ending, Losing, Letting Go, The Neutral Zone, and New Beginning. They recommend engagement and support and using additional change management tools from other methods to enhance.[19]

5. **CAP™ by GE**—Change Acceleration Process (CAP) is no longer used by GE, yet this method still has fans and people who continue to use it. It uses a three-phase approach: current state, transition state, and future state, and a five-step process. Each step contains planning tools, deliverables, activities, and assessments.[20]

6. **Kotter's 8 Step Model**—Uses a three-phase approach: creating a climate for change, engaging and enabling the organization, and implementing and sustaining for change, and the eight steps. Planning tools, deliverables, activities, and assessments are peppered throughout the steps.[21]

7. **The Standard for Change Management by ACMP**— Uses a five-area approach: evaluating change impacts and organization readiness, formulating change management strategy, developing change management plans, executing change management plans, and closing change management effort. Each area contains planning tools, deliverables, activities, and assessments.[22]

8. **Your Organization**—Most consulting firms and many large organizations have leveraged these models and customized methods for their own needs. In my opinion, a customized approach is almost always the best approach. Having said that, I have seen a dozen custom methodologies and have made a few myself. Guess what? They all contain a few phases, some steps, and planning tools, deliverables, activities, and assessments.

The important wisdom to gain from this chapter is that all of our top methodologies are very similar in structure and design. If you take more time to dig deeper, you will see that many of our planning tools, deliverables, activities, and assessments are a lot alike as well. This is because we are change people and we know that our best results are gained when we customize our work for our stakeholders.

Supporting the stakeholders through their change experience means that nothing out of the box works exceptionally well for anyone.

At HNH, I streamlined our methodology into four familiar categories of work and then put our planning tools, deliverables, activities, and assessments in each category. I used the process phases that the EHR implementation was using (no need for competing tech terms) and eliminated any extra step names (no need to be confusing). Our methodology was born from a scoping exercise and is shown below in Table 18.1.

Table 18.1   Change Adoption Scope

	Key Area	Description
1	**Diagnostics and alignment**	Activities and deliverables to scope the magnitude of change, allocate budget, and align the change initiative to the organization's strategic direction.
2	**Communications**	All change initiative related communication planning, design, development, delivery, and feedback processing. Open communication channel directly to project team.
3	**Leadership and engagement**	All leadership change skill development, leadership support for leading a change initiative, leadership readiness programs (design, development, and execution). Engagement planning, events, coordination, and materials for distribution. Go-live support activities for project and stakeholders.
4	**Adoption measurement**	Measurements, distribution, and reporting for readiness for change, effective change engagement, and go-live change adoption.

Other innovations at HNH improved our team performance and included:

- Branding the change effort "Change and Adoption" to promote the desired end state of adoption.
- Simplifying planning and tool documentation to make certain all leaders, program team members, and employees understood the methods and tools used to support adoption.
- Creating Readiness Programs for inpatient, outpatient, lab, revenue cycle, and providers.
- Measuring leader and employee readiness for adoption at regular intervals. These measurements were shared broadly to help identify units requiring additional support.

Call to action!
Starting to think you might need some change adoption support? Find Dr. Keely Killpack on LinkedIn to connect to the global network of change professionals!

Chapter 19

Change Adoption Basic Toolkit

I have literally shared almost all of our change adoption professional trade secrets in this section! It feels good and I have always believed that sharing what you know is the way to go! I want readers to know what change adoption professionals do, what we are like, and that our methods are rooted in science. We are not half as mysterious as people think, but we are twice as creative!

Some of our best assets are the tools we have to help articulate a change and our support elements that help people through the change experience. I have assembled a few tools to create the **Change Adoption Basic Toolkit** for helping to adopt change.

The **Change Adoption Basic Toolkit** contains 14 tools, which are additions to the previous **Executive Sponsor** and **Change Essentials Toolkits**. If you are going to be supporting a change initiative as a change adoption professional, I would expect you to use the tools in all three toolkits. If you're already a seasoned change adoption professional, you likely have your own iterations of these same tools.

As a refresher, the **Executive Sponsor Toolkit** contains three tools for scoping the magnitude of change and assessing change risk. They are described in Table 19.1.

The **Change Essentials Toolkit** contains eight tools that provide simple, consumable formats for change initiative projects. These tools help stakeholders begin their change journey and can be created by leaders or people on project teams making changes (Table 19.2).

Table 19.1 Executive Sponsor Change Toolkit

	Tool	*Description*
1	3-Legged stool	Tool used to illustrate the scope of change in three common areas: People, Process, and Technology. Questions help drive answers and the tool can be used in any initial discussion of the change.
2	Change risk quick query	Survey tools used to scope the complexity of the people side of the change. Questions help determine change resource needs and change readiness of the organization at the beginning.
3	Change heat map	Planning tool to inform leaders of the competitive landscape surrounding the change initiative.

Note: Executive Sponsor Change Toolkit is available in full color download at http://www.ChangeRxBook.com.

Table 19.2 Change Essentials Toolkit

	Tool	*Description*
1	Project vision	A short, compelling elevator speech about the change initiative, its importance, and benefits to the organization and employees.
2	Stakeholder circle	A visual way to identify each of the audiences impacted by the changes coming that helps groups know they are important and on your radar.
3	Meeting invite	A simple Outlook Calendar template that helps leaders and project teams engage audiences in change activities. You will be setting up a lot of meetings and asking people to take a lot of time out of their days to meet with you. It's important to engage them and express gratitude for their time and energy.
4	Timeline— high level	A simple, high level view of the timeline for the change initiative. It is used to kick off the change and again at multiple points to help context setting or to remind groups of where we are in the big picture.
5	Timeline— mid level	A little more specific view of the timeline for the change initiative. It provides a few more details for various audience groups, depending on their change experience. It helps to illustrate complexity and gives a bit clearer of a picture of what is going to happen along the way.
6	Timeline— key activities	A detailed view of the activities or events that audience groups will experience. It doesn't show all of the work plan details, but does detail work that anyone in operations should expect to participate in, hear about, or know about.

(Continued)

Table 19.2 (Continued)   Change Essentials Toolkit

	Tool	Description
7	Milestone tracker	The most detailed view of all the readiness activities and milestones that involve operations. It lists everything operational leaders should keep track of, care about, or need to know. It helps leaders see the time and effort they will need to dedicate to this change and owners of activities.
8	Milestone calendar	This is the same detail as the Milestone Tracker, just shown in calendar format instead of listing activities by month. It is very helpful for posting on an office or break room wall to keep track of all the activities going on to get ready for a change implementation.

Note: Change Essentials Toolkit is available in full color download at http://www.ChangeRxBook.com.

The **Change Adoption Basic Toolkit** contains 14 additional tools that change adoption professionals should always have at the ready. Table 19.3 describes each one briefly. A breakout section is also provided for each of the tools with samples and additional detail. The entire collection of tools in the Change Essentials Toolkit is available to download in full color and tool templates include the samples seen here along with easy-to-follow instructions for creating your own.

Table 19.3 Change Adoption Basic Toolkit

	Tool	*Description*
1	Change adoption methodology	Simple methodology graphic and description of elements, plan, and overview of adapted or leveraged theories
2	Change roadmap	Timeline of change deliverables across change initiative
3	Change curve tool	Fun graphic tool to approach discussion on change experience with stakeholders and used to help describe and assess the change experience
4	Leader checklist	Monthly checklist for leaders to track and record readiness activities
5	Talking points	Executive handout distributed at go-live events to support leaders
6	Handout	Action-oriented handout that facilitates leading and supporting change
7	Communication inventory	Activity used to identify the best practice communication channels for your audience/organization
8	Communication channels	Results of inventory activity, sets expectations for communication planning and confirms decision making
9	Email	Brief, consumable, mission-centric emails to facilitate change or reinforce desired behaviors

(*Continued*)

Table 19.3 (Continued)   Change Adoption Basic Toolkit

	Tool	*Description*
10	Article	Engaging, concise article to diverse audience groups to garner interest around change or drive awareness
11	Adoption measure—leader readiness	Fun, simple survey to measure leaders' feelings and attitudes for implementation
12	Adoption measure—executive rounding	Fun, simple form for executives to record feedback and insights while rounding during go-live periods
13	Adoption measure—super user shift	Fun, simple form for super users to record feedback and insights from their support shifts during go-live periods
14	Adoption report	Daily report out of data gathered from executives and super user adoption measures

Note: Change Adoption Basic Toolkit is available in full color download at http://www.ChangeRxBook.com.

19.1 TOOL #1 Change Adoption Methodology

The **Change Adoption Methodology** is a simple framework represented in a clean, easy graphic to help leaders, stakeholders, and project team members better understand your work. At the beginning of a change initiative, you will be meeting with lots of groups, helping them understand your role, your work, and why it adds value.

19.2 SAMPLE #1 Change Adoption Methodology

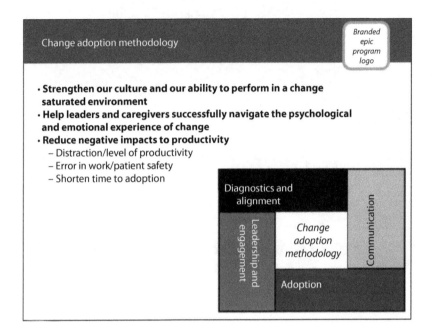

19.3 TOOL #2 Change Roadmap

The **Change Roadmap** is an easy way to show the change adoption deliverables and activities across a change initiative timeline. It helps any audience realize the work you will be doing while other members of a project are doing their work. It is also separated by the four categories of the change adoption methodology, which helps audiences see your work activities.

19.4 SAMPLE #2 Change Roadmap

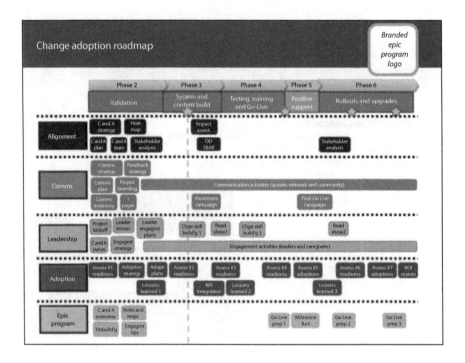

19.5 TOOL #3 Change Curve

The **Change Curve** is the most famous of all change tools! It originated from Kubler-Ross and this version is adapted from Prosci's ADKAR™ model at HNH. The change curve helps explain the emotional, nonlinear journey of change adoption. It can be useful for employees to identify where they are in the journey, or to use at important milestones. A word of caution though; since most employees experience multiple changes occurring at the same time, this tool is almost obsolete. If it's helpful, use it. If you have five change curves for each employee, it will become overwhelming for everyone.

19.6 SAMPLE #3 Change Curve

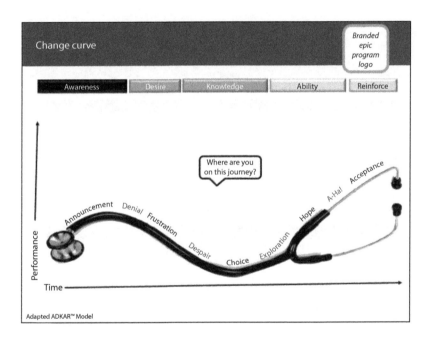

19.7 TOOL #4 Leader Checklist

The **Leader Checklist** is an essential tool during any large-scale change. Published monthly, they help all leaders keep track of their readiness activities and stay engaged. This version was branded like the milestone tracker, and these tools were delivered in a package each month. The checklist was coveted and leveraged by about 200 leaders at HNH for more than a year!

19.8 SAMPLE #4 Leaders Checklist

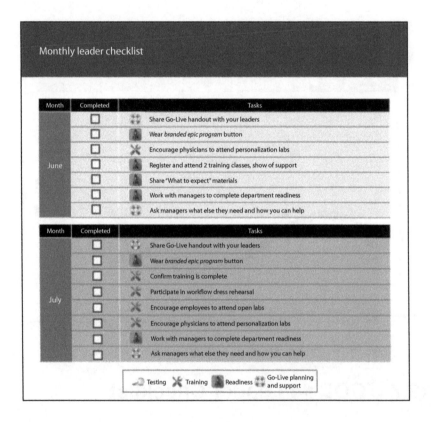

19.9 TOOL #5 Leader Talking Points

The **Leader Talking Points** are behavior themes and statements. They were intended for leaders who would be rounding HNH's facilities during go-live events. It was important that executives and leaders had consistent messaging and would have the right things to say in most circumstances. The talking points were reviewed in go-live orientations and also provided at the beginning of each rounding shift. Small, pocket card versions were made for super users and employees, and the leader version was a simple page size (they had to carry a clipboard while rounding so this size was easy).

19.10 SAMPLE #5 Leader Talking Points

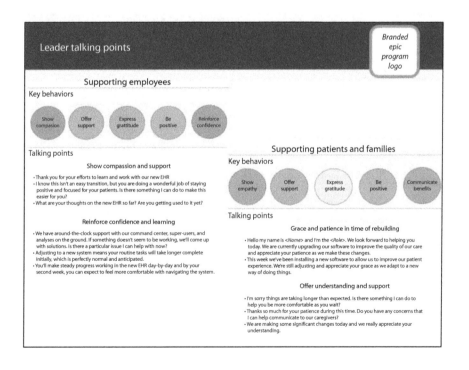

19.11 TOOL #6 Handout

The **Handout** was used as an action-oriented change piece. It was used during a leadership change capability workshop, designed to help leaders strengthen their change skills. The handout was a contest among leaders and was a fun, engaging way to interact, learn about the change, and realize what skills they would need to leverage to lead their teams to adoption.

19.12 SAMPLE #6 Handout

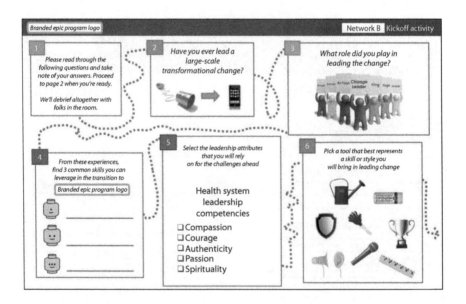

19.13 TOOL #7 Communication Inventory

The **Communication Inventory** is an activity used to identify the best practice communication methods and channels for your organization and stakeholder groups. It's an engaging way to ensure you plan to deliver messages in the channels and formats that are effective for your audience and feasible to your organization.

19.14 SAMPLE #7 Communication Inventory

Internal communication inventory					
Network	Community	Publication	Audience	Vehicle	Frequency
Network A	One hospital	Online news digest	All employees	Email	Daily (M–F)
		eNews	All employees	Printed	Update as needed
		eShare	Leadership	Email	As needed
		eAnswers	Leadership	Email	As needed
		Online news source	Physicians	Email constant contact	As needed at medical executive request
		Volunteer vitals	Volunteer and friends	Print and email via online news sources. Mailed directly to homes.	Monthly
		Wellness email	Employees in wellness programs	Email	Usually weekly
Network B	One hospital	Online news source	All employees	Email	Every Friday
		Leadership messages	Leadership	Email	As needed
		Departmental mailings and flyers for announcements	All employees	Printed	Update as needed
		Volunteer and auxiliary newsletters	Volunteers	Printed	Monthly or quarterly
	Two hospitals	Online news source	All employees	Email	As needed
		FYI	All employees	Email	As needed
	Three hospitals	Online news source	All employees	Email	Payday Friday
		Volunteer and auxiliary newsletters	Volunteers	Printed	Monthly or quarterly
	Four hospitals	Online news source	All employees	Email	Aprox once a month
Labs	Laboratories	Online news source	All lab employees	Email	Every Wednesday before noon

19.15 TOOL #8 Communication Channels

The **Communication Channels** illustrates the results of the communication inventory. It is used to confirm decision making and set expectations for communication planning. It reinforces how and where stakeholder groups will receive information from your change initiative, as well as the ways they will be able to submit feedback or questions.

19.16 SAMPLE #8 Communication Channels

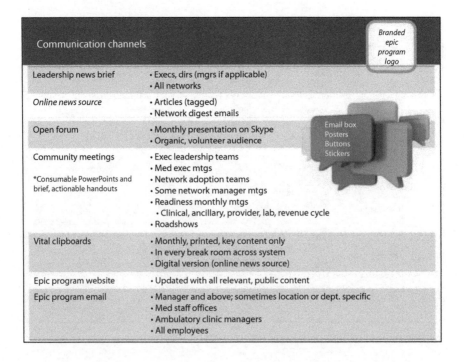

Communication channels		Branded epic program logo
Leadership news brief	• Execs, dirs (mgrs if applicable) • All networks	
Online news source	• Articles (tagged) • Network digest emails	
Open forum	• Monthly presentation on Skype • Organic, volunteer audience	Email box Posters Buttons Stickers
Community meetings *Consumable PowerPoints and brief, actionable handouts	• Exec leadership teams • Med exec mtgs • Network adoption teams • Some network manager mtgs • Readiness monthly mtgs • Clinical, ancillary, provider, lab, revenue cycle • Roadshows	
Vital clipboards	• Monthly, printed, key content only • In every break room across system • Digital version (online news source)	
Epic program website	• Updated with all relevant, public content	
Epic program email	• Manager and above; sometimes location or dept. specific • Med staff offices • Ambulatory clinic managers • All employees	

19.17 TOOL #9 Email

The **Email** is the least effective yet most common communication tool these days. It's important to keep change initiative emails branded similarly, with a tone of gratitude and always reminding readers of the elevator story and the value of the coming change. The versions provided below show the evolution to being more engaging, visually interesting, and more concise.

19.18 SAMPLE #9 Email

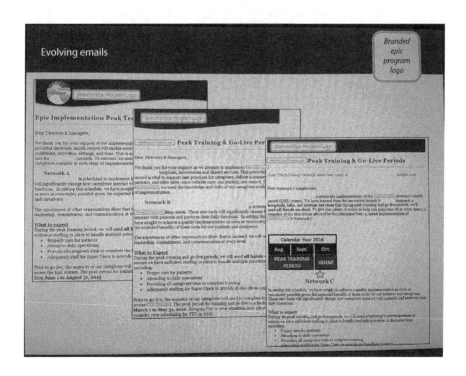

19.19 TOOL #10 Article

Publishing online **Article** was fun and engaging for the creators and the readers! They always take more thought and time than you realize, but a concise article to diverse audience groups that garners interest around the change or drive awareness is always more effective than another email.

19.20 SAMPLE #10 Article

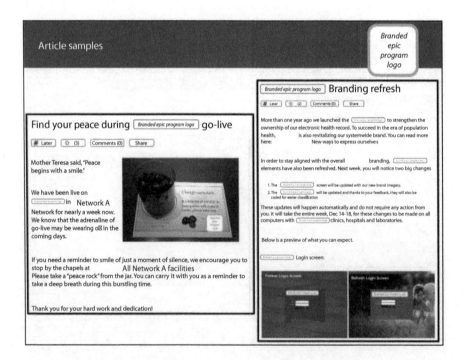

19.21 TOOL #11 Adoption Measure— Leader Readiness

The **Adoption Measure—Leader Readiness** was designed to help leaders realize what they need to do in order to gain confidence and be ready for the change. It was a simple survey to measure leaders' feelings and attitudes. We distributed in paper form at significant project milestone meetings, collected them upon exit, and reported the collated results to the senior executive team.

19.22 SAMPLE #11 Adoption Measure—Leader Readiness

Adoption measure—leader readiness				*Branded epic program logo*

Branded epic program logo

Go Live readiness assessment 60 day-leader readiness assessment
We would appreciate your honest feedback below. Your input will help us better support the changes coming with *branded epic program*. **Please use the back to** tell us how we can help more.
Your name: _____
Please print

A ready leader...			
Understands the *branded epic program* timeline and critical activities and communicated regularly			
Sets an example for personal commitment and accountability for implementation success			
Monitors critical readiness activities, publically acknowledging progress and accomplishments			
Manages competing work to help create focus for caregivers during implementation			
Creates availability and an environment where staff feel it is safe to ask questions or discuss problems			
Is present and actively supports caregivers during training and go-live			
Has arranged personal and professional life to accomodate go-live demands			
Responds effectively to escalated issues, removing barriers and addressing critical concerns in a timely and constructive manner.			
Speaks positively and confidently about *branded epic program* to managers, caregivers and patients			
Is knowledgeable about the impact of *branded epic program* on workflows, policies and procedures			

19.23 TOOL #12 Adoption Measure—Executive Rounding

The **Adoption Measure—Executive Rounding** was an intentionally fun and simple form for executives to record feedback and insights while rounding during go-live periods. They needed an eye catching form to jot notes and record things they were observing. This form helped keep the executives engaged in the process and provided great content for articles and adoption reporting.

19.24 SAMPLE #12 Adoption Measure—Executive Rounding

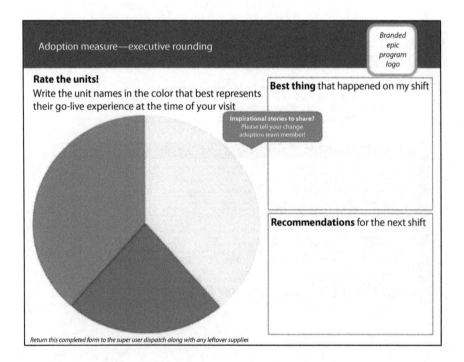

19.25 TOOL #13 Adoption Measure—Super User Shift

The **Adoption Measure—Super User Shift** was also an intentionally fun and simple form for super users to record feedback and insights from their support shifts during go-live periods. Similarly, they appreciated the eye catching form to jot notes and record things they were observing. It also provided great content for articles and adoption reporting.

19.26 SAMPLE #13 Adoption Measure—Super User Shift

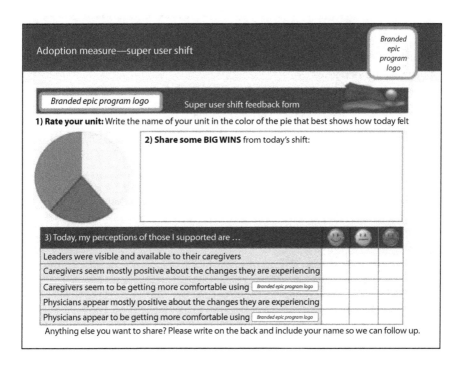

19.27 TOOL #14 Adoption Report

The **Adoption Report** was included in the change initiative's daily report. The report covered people, processes, and technology, each of their respective successes and challenges, and was distributed to the entire organization each day. Our adoption measures fed this content for the daily adoption report. From the samples below you can see some days include quotes and moods; others just had the representative data.

19.28 SAMPLE #14 Adoption Report

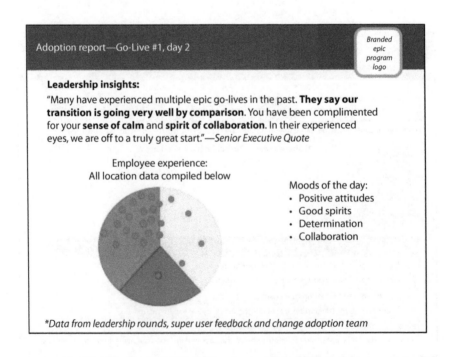

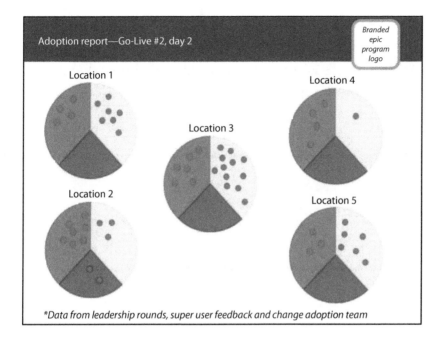

The 14 tools showcased above in this Change Adoption Basic Toolkit are just some of the very effective tools needed to support any change initiative. To make change adoption faster and easier, you need to be able to tell the story of the change in a consumable way. You need to give people the information they need, as they need it, in a way that reduces fear and increases confidence in the change. Change adoption professionals also use a lot of planning tools, meeting presentations, communication elements, and so much more. This collection can help you quickly distribute some of the fundamentals of the trade, and the tools provide the thinking behind these and instructions to quickly distribute your own.

Inspired by something you read?
Tweet about it **@DrKeelyK** or **#ChangeRxBook**

VII

BEST PRACTICES FOR SUCCESSFUL CHANGE ADOPTION

Chapter 20—Seven Concepts to Remember

Overview: This section provides some broad reaching insights and wisdom about successfully adopting change.

Your Prescription for Leading Change: Here are some immediate steps you can take to adopt the ideas in this section.

- Write down the name(s) of people you know or have heard of who are change management professionals. Use my name if you're drawing a blank. Look them up on LinkedIn. If you see change skills or similar descriptions of work like you have read here, connect with them. It is highly likely you will need their advice or support in the near future.

Chapter 20

Seven Concepts to Remember

Oftentimes, best practices are realized after the fact. That's why most people reflect on their work, ask for feedback, solicit for lessons learned, or generate after action reports. Reflecting and learning from our past experiences is one of the best practices anyone can do on any job.

After reflecting, gathering feedback from others, and analyzing all the different aspects of my work and my team's efforts, I have realized there are seven very important, fundamental things that made all the difference to our success.

1. **Change adoption success was really everyone's success.** My team's work, our unique contributions and psychological support, helped make change faster and easier for close to 10,000 leaders, physicians, and employees at Healing Neighbors Healthcare (HNH). While we were implementing a new electronic health record (EHR) system, we were also standardizing the

work processes for all of our operational staff, and creating an enterprise standard for leading, communicating, and supporting large-scale changes. So many benefits were realized from our change adoption team's performance:

– **Financial**—Hundreds of thousands of dollars in savings from reduced staffing and support costs during go-lives. Some may not attribute this directly to our work, but the evidence is clear and all of it correlates to our change adoption methodology and measured outcomes:

  • **Technical issues** were resolved significantly faster because of the collaborative and positive attitudes of the people working to solve them.

  • **Physicians and employees** openly leveraged the expert super users to ensure they were using the new system correctly, until they didn't need them anymore.

  • **Leaders** were highly engaged and could see that the system was working, the new processes made sense, and their people were adopting the changes and were able to do that with less and less support very quickly.

– **Leaders**—Leaders developed change competency and improved communication skills, so the next time around every leader will be better equipped to help with change adoption. For the first time at HNH, leaders also reported feeling connected to colleagues in other locations and valued those connections for additional support.

- **Physicians**—Hundreds of physicians who practice at Healing Neighbors Healthcare (HNH) experienced change support and transitioned to computerized order entry faster and easier than anyone expected. Most attributed this to their readiness for the change and the helpful, positive attitudes of all the staff encouraging the change.
- **Company culture**—Positivity, collaboration, and trust were increased significantly due to transparency and more effective communication elements developed and distributed via our change adoption team.
- **Corporate communications**—Our enterprise communication plan was the first of its kind and the change adoption levers we included in all of our communications became part of the standard for HNH. Our EHR program communications also helped launch HNH's company intranet; driving employees from all locations to one common platform for their news, announcements, employee links, and company media.
- **Learning and development**—A required leadership development course (Leading Teams through Change) was co-created and facilitated by my team of experts and delivered to hundreds of leaders across all locations.

2. **Why we are changing cannot be overstated enough.**
   To ensure any change is adopted as quickly and easily
   as possible, it needs to be something everyone can see
   is worthwhile. We created powerful and direct messaging that reminded leaders, physicians, and employees
   about our organization's mission, vision, and core val-
   ues. Equally important was to communicate how this
   strategic priority supported our fundamental identity.
   We made sure that our Epic EHR implementation
   was seamlessly connected to our overall strategic
   priorities and that every communication we shared
   in the first year included just a couple of sentences
   to remind readers of why we are doing this work
   and how it connects to the big picture. We also supported a few other large change projects and each
   of those also leveraged this technique. It is so much
   easier to engage employees in a change if you can
   clearly articulate why it is important and the benefits
   they will reap.

3. **Assume good intent and trust others.** In any
   change initiative, it takes multiple leaders making decisions and many hands working together for success.
   Inevitably some things don't go according to plan or
   people don't see things in the same way all the time.
   In moments where we drift apart or expectations are
   not met, it is best to assume good intent. If someone
   is acting in a way that doesn't make any sense or isn't
   performing as you expect, assume they are a good
   person, doing their best, acting in the way they think

is right. When you come from a place of good intent, it is easier to try to understand the situation and correct it. When you trust that people are doing their best and that they are after the same success as you are, it creates a more supportive way to correct behavior. Leaders especially have to trust that people on their teams are doing their best work and are capable of doing it right. If people doubt their direction or ability, but we make it easy to talk about or ask for clarity, they will inevitably use their good intent and reach out for help.

4. **Equal partnerships and clarifying roles.** Our Electronic Health Record (EHR) implementation involved people, processes, and technology changes. Each of those changes had many milestones, activities, and separate teams, which had to be coordinated together in time. In our change initiative and in many more success stories just like it, having equal partnerships among the leaders of the people, processes, and technology work efforts is the best approach. When these three areas are all interdependent, it works best to have all the leaders collaborating and working together. In our case, we integrated our work plans, had daily huddles to ensure we stayed together on decision making and problem solving, and had a collaborative approach to our executive sponsor, senior executive team, steering committee, and board of directors. This equal partnership was also important because sometimes the work overlaps, people's responsibilities can

be misunderstood, or a challenge in one area impacts the others and needs a solution to mitigate all areas. Creating an extensive roles and responsibilities document can be very helpful, but direct and frequent partnership is still the best.

5. **Physicians have unique change needs and require dedicated resources.** It is common knowledge that physicians are a unique stakeholder group in healthcare. They have unique employment relationships (employee, contracted, community, privileged at multiple locations, solely independent, etc.), and their change experience is also more complex than other groups because of the range of changes for each specialty and physician type. At HNH, there was a dedicated Physician Change Support Team who supported the physician experience. The group included the Chief Medical Information Officer (CMIO), a handful of Physician Champions from various specialties, the Health Informatics Physician Liaison, the Clinical Content and Decision Support Physician Lead, our Change Adoption Provider Professional, and the Training Lead for Physician Curriculum. What was so effective about our experience was the collaboration among this group, the support they gave each other, and the myriad of ways they were able to engage with physicians of all types leading up to implementation. Together, this group facilitated Physician Readiness Programs in all locations, attended handfuls of Medical Staff events, hosted open lab hours in private physician lounges to be conveniently available to doctors

at any time, and did endless hours of rounding and talking specifically to physicians about their change experience. We also provided DocTalk, an email just for physicians answering their questions and channeling important information to them. Physicians have so many complex change needs, and it was invaluable to have a change adoption resource planning and tracking all the nuances, as well as preparing communication and presentation materials that really targeted information to this audience.

6. **Silos only exist on paper; change changes everyone.** Our EHR implementation reached almost everyone who worked within Healing Neighbors Healthcare, in varying ways, at varying times, and with varying levels of engagement. All of this complexity in the change experience meant that the collaboration was essential; for almost everybody. We see this interconnectedness comes up in all kinds of ways in the world today. Medication interactions, chronic disease influencing more than one system, the way our smartphones track our location and traffic and can give us smart advice about travel. It's important to begin to shift our thinking to a broader, strategic view for a lot of things. If one group of stakeholders needs something, it's likely other groups do also. If something worked really well, repeat it and keep doing it until everyone gets to experience it. If two departments are both focused on developing leadership skills, working together to double the value of that learning experience is the best approach.

It takes more time and energy to collaborate and to think of the bigger implications of your work, but it is worth it. Developing collaborative approaches with other departments that are also supporting people and their work experience is a very worthwhile investment if you are involved in a change initiative.

7. **Relationships make all the difference.** At any company undergoing change, everyone's footing will be loose at times. We rely on each other for information sharing, support, compassion, power and influence, and professional development. Building strong, trusting relationships with people who influence your work (or whose work you influence) is a very, very good idea. Good relationships with the right partners make the work easier, successes more likely, and the work experience more positive. They can even increase your level of commitment to your job and the people around you. Kindness, positivity, and demonstrating competency in your work go a long way in establishing good relationships.

Change. It's everywhere and now it is constant. Change adoption professionals are highly skilled and have proven tools to help make change initiatives faster and easier to adopt. In an attempt to demystify our industry, I have provided history, science, stories and samples of our work. Anyone in a position to change healthcare should feel empowered to start leveraging these types of tools and techniques right away.

I have provided prescriptions for my most common types of patients and if you take these and keep using them, I promise you'll get better at making adoption faster and easier. I hope you gained valuable insights from reading this book, and it was fun and engaging along the way. Best of luck on all the change journeys ahead of you!

Inspired by something you read?
Tweet about it **@DrKeelyK** or **#ChangeRxBook**

Appendix

Adoption: The act of mastering a new behavior or skill and having it become the standard way a person behaves.

Affordable Care Act (ACA): Also known as Obamacare. A U.S. federal statute enacted by President Barack Obama in 2010. Together with the Health Care and Education Reconciliation Act amendment, it represents the most significant regulatory overhaul of the U.S. healthcare system since the passage of Medicare and Medicaid in 1965. Under the act, hospitals and primary physicians would transform their practices financially, technologically, and clinically to drive better health outcomes, lower costs, and improve their methods of distribution and accessibility.[23]

Change Adoption: This author's term for "Change Management." The global industry and formal practice of helping companies and their *employees* adopt a new way of operating. The formal definition is "Change management is a structured approach to transitioning individuals, teams, and organizations from a current state to a desired future state. It is an organizational process aimed at empowering employees to accept and embrace changes in their current business environment."[24]

Change Adoption Basic Toolkit: A collection of 14 tools for Change Adoption Professionals who are supporting a change initiative. Includes Change Adoption Methodology, Change Roadmap, Change Curve Tool, Leader Checklist, Talking Points, Handout, Communication Inventory, Communication Channels, Email, Article, Adoption Measure—Leader Readiness, Adoption Measure—Executive Rounding, Adoption Measure—Super User Shift, and Adoption Report.

Change Essentials Toolkit: A collection of eight tools for leaders and people on projects making change. Includes Project Vision, Stakeholder Circle, Meeting Invite, Timeline—High Level, Timeline—Mid Level, Timeline—Key Activities, Milestone Tracker, and Milestone Calendar.

Change Initiative: Any project, program, or initiative that requires *people* to do their jobs differently in some significant way(s).

Change Management: The global industry and formal practice of helping companies and their *employees* adopt a new way of operating. Change management is a structured approach to transitioning individuals, teams, and organizations from a current state to a desired future state. It is an organizational process aimed at empowering employees to accept and embrace changes in their current business environment.[24]

Change Transformation: When a business significantly alters its normal operations. Usually a large-scale effort to mobilize the workforce to do their work in new and different ways.

Deployment: In the business context, the body of work required to implement or install a new business solution in a company's operations.

Executive Sponsor Change Toolkit: A collection of three tools for Executive Sponsors leading a change initiative. Includes 3-Legged Stool, Change Risk Quick Query, and Change Heat Map.

Healing Neighbors Healthcare (HNH): The pseudonym given to the large-scale transformational change initiative case study of a health system that implemented Epic's electronic health record system.

Health Informatics: The interdisciplinary study of the design, development, adoption, and application of IT-based innovations in healthcare services delivery, management, and planning.[25]

Implementation: In the business context, the body of work required to deploy or install a new business solution in a company's operations.

Milestone: Typically a consulting term, a milestone is an event or activity in a project that marks progress toward implementation.

Obamacare: An alternative name for the Affordable Care Act (ACA). A U.S. federal statute enacted by President Barack Obama in 2010. Together with the Health Care and Education Reconciliation Act amendment, it represents the most significant regulatory overhaul of the U.S. healthcare system since the passage of Medicare and Medicaid in 1965. Under the act, hospitals and primary care physicians would transform their practices financially, technologically, and clinically to drive better health outcomes, lower costs, and improve their methods of distribution and accessibility.[26]

Rx: The Latin abbreviation for medical prescription. A prescription is a healthcare program implemented by a physician or other qualified healthcare practitioner in the form of instructions that govern the plan of care for an individual patient.[27]

Transformational Change: When a business significantly alters its normal operations. Usually a large-scale effort to mobilize the workforce to do their work in new and different ways.

References

1. https://www.prosci.com/change-management/thought-leadership-library/change-management-definition
2. http://www.moravian.org/wp-content/uploads/2013/06/Bridges_Transition_Model.pdf
3. https://en.wikipedia.org/wiki/Epic_Systems
4. http://www.imdb.com/title/tt1417592/
5. https://www.psychologytoday.com/blog/brain-wise/201606/emotions-are-contagious
6. https://www.tutorialspoint.com/management_concepts/the_rule_of_seven.htm
7. http://www.torbenrick.eu/blog/change-management/12-reasons-why-people-resist-change/
8. https://www.google.com/webhp?sourceid=chrome-instant&rlz=1C1NDCM_enUS705US706&ion=1&espv=2&ie=UTF-8#q=definition%20of%20burnout
9. http://www.mayoclinicproceedings.org/article/S0025-6196(15)00716-8/abstract
10. http://emedicine.medscape.com/article/806779-overview
11. https://en.wikipedia.org/wiki/Industrial_Revolution
12. http://www.change-management-coach.com/kubler-ross.html
13. http://www.managementstudyguide.com/goal-setting-theory-motivation.htm
14. https://en.wikipedia.org/wiki/Goal_setting
15. https://en.wikipedia.org/wiki/Social_cognitive_theory
16. https://www.prosci.com/adkar
17. http://www.imaworldwide.com/change-management-methodology/installation-v-implementation
18. https://www.beingfirst.com/services/change-leaders-roadmap-methodology/

19. https://www.mindtools.com/pages/article/bridges-transition-model.htm
20. http://www.slideshare.net/HomerZhang/ge-change-managementcap
21. http://www.kotterinternational.com/the-8-step-process-for-leading-change/
22. http://c.ymcdn.com/sites/www.acmpglobal.org/resource/resmgr/standard_info_brochure.pdf
23. https://en.wikipedia.org/wiki/Patient_Protection_and_Affordable_Care_Act
24. http://en.wikipedia.org/wiki/Change_management
25. https://en.wikipedia.org/wiki/Health_informatics
26. https://en.wikipedia.org/wiki/Patient_Protection_and_Affordable_Care_Act
27. https://en.wikipedia.org/wiki/Medical_prescription

Index